2nd Edition

Training Design
BASICS

Saul Carliner

atd
PRESS

ATD Press is an internationally renowned source of insightful and practical information on talent development, training, and professional development.

ATD Press
1640 King Street
Alexandria, VA 22314 USA

Ordering information: Books published by ATD Press can be purchased by visiting ATD's website at www.td.org/books or by calling 800.628.2783 or 703.683.8100.

Library of Congress Control Number: 2015947321

ISBN-10: 1-56286-925-6
ISBN-13: 978-1-56286-925-0
e-ISBN: 978-1-60728-500-7

ATD Press Editorial Staff
Director: Kristine Luecker
Manager: Christian Green
Community of Practice Manager, Learning & Development: Amanda Smith
Developmental Editor: Jack Harlow
Cover Design: Fatimah Weller
Text Design: Maggie Hyde and Tony Julien
Printed by Data Reproductions Corporation, Auburn Hills, MI

Contents

About the Training Basics Series

ATD's Training Basics series recognizes and, in some ways, celebrates the fast-paced, ever-changing reality of organizations today. Jobs, roles, and expectations change quickly. One day you might be a network administrator or a process line manager, and the next day you might be asked to train 50 employees in basic computer skills or to instruct line workers in quality processes.

Where do you turn for help? The ATD Training Basics series is designed to be your one-stop solution. The series takes a minimalist approach to your learning curve dilemma and presents only the information you need to be successful. Each book in the series guides you through key aspects of training: giving presentations, making the transition to the role of trainer, designing and delivering training, and evaluating training. The books in the series also include some advanced skills, such as performance and basic business proficiencics.

The ATD Training Basics series is the perfect tool for training and performance professionals looking for easy-to-understand materials that will prepare nontrainers to take on a training role. In addition, this series is the consummate reference tool for any trainer's bookshelf and a quick way to hone your existing skills.

Preface

Training Design Basics explains how to design and develop training programs, primarily those programs intended for the face-to-face or virtual classroom. It also provides guidance for designing and developing self-study training programs, such as online tutorials and workbooks.

Many training design books focus almost exclusively on the analysis and evaluation phases of creating training programs. This one gives as much attention to the design, development, and implementation phases, exploring issues such as how to structure a program (including the parts of every program that would not appear in an outline), choose an instructional strategy, determine which materials you need to develop (such as student and instructor guides for classroom courses), follow clear writing and visual design guidelines for these materials, and conduct a review to ensure that the draft program is likely to achieve its objectives.

This book also focuses on designing and developing these programs in the real world, in which trainers make do with limited time, funds, and other resources. Yes, trainers have to analyze needs and write objectives. After all, trainers need to know what they are training and what the resulting program should accomplish. But trainers often have limited time to get this information and some of the key sources of information are not always available. So this book suggests ways to adjust the effort of gathering and assessing information about a project, a process called *analysis*, to the realities in which trainers work.

Similarly, although tutorials and other forms of instruction receive much attention in the training press, the majority of training still takes place in the classroom. Therefore, this book focuses primarily on designing and developing classroom programs, while also addressing the design and development of technology-delivered programs.

Finally, after designing and developing training programs, many trainers are responsible for launching and running their programs. This book explores these tasks, too, especially as they relate to administering, marketing, and supporting training programs.

Who Should Read This Book

Training Design Basics guides people who have never designed a training program through their first project. It is intended for new course developers and instructors; subject matter experts (SMEs) thrust into training roles; and other nontrainers who find themselves responsible for designing and developing training programs.

How This Book Is Organized

Chapter 1 "The Basics of Designing Training Programs" introduces issues to consider when designing training programs, such as the general concepts of learning (and its distinction from information sharing), human performance improvement, and adult learning

Chapter 2 "The Basics of Planning a Training Project" provides an overview of the process for designing training programs and suggests ways to answer the question "how much time is needed to design and develop a training program?" before you start developing it. This chapter also describes the roles that people play in a training project and suggests ways to effectively work with sponsors.

Chapter 3 "The Basic Information Needed to Start a Project" describes the first part of the analysis phase of instructional design: gathering information. This chapter identifies the information needed to design a training project and why you need that information, and offers suggestions on how to get that information when you have a tight schedule.

Chapter 4 "The Basic Instructional Objective" describes the second part of the analysis phase of instructional design: defining requirements. This chapter explains how to concretely state the goals of a training program and how to assess whether learners have achieved those goals (a step you perform before beginning to design programs).

Chapter 5 "The Basics of Organizing Training Programs" explains the general structure of a program, and how to divide content into units. This chapter delves into the most popular formats (live, self-study) and communication media (classroom, computer) for training programs.

Chapter 6 "The Basics of Choosing an Instructional Strategy" explores a variety of ways to present instructional material so that it engages learners and they retain it.

Chapter 7 "The Basics of Developing Instructional Materials" identifies the types of materials you must develop for training programs, including student materials, slides, and instructor's notes for classroom and self-study courses.

Chapter 8 "The Basics of Preparing and Producing Instructional Materials" describes the guidelines for writing and designing these instructional materials, as well as considerations for producing them.

Chapter 9 "The Basic Quality Checks for Training Programs" explains how to conduct reviews and pilot tests to ensure the accuracy and effectiveness of instructional materials before you make them available to others.

Chapter 10 "The Basics of Administering Training Programs" clarifies the responsibilities of course designers and developers after a course goes public.

Each chapter opens with a quick access guide—What's Inside This Chapter—to introduce you to the contents of the chapter. Use this section to identify the information it contains and, if you wish, skip ahead to the material most useful to you.

The final section of each chapter—Getting It Done—offers you a chance to practice some of the concepts discussed in the chapter and provides closing tips and pointers to help you apply what you have learned.

This book strives to make it as easy as possible for you to understand and apply its lessons. Icons throughout the book help you identify key points to retain.

Basic Rules

These rules cut to the chase. They are unequivocal and important concepts for facilitators.

Noted

This icon is used to give you more detail or explanation about a concept or a principle. It is also occasionally used for a short but productive tangent.

Think About This

These are helpful tips to help you prepare for facilitation or during facilitation.

What's New in This Edition?

Although the overall structure and basic approach to designing training programs described in this second edition of *Training Design Basics* has remained the same, the book has been updated throughout to reflect changes in training practice since the publication of the first edition. The major changes include:

- The book now addresses live virtual classes and online tutorials, in addition to face-to-face classes and self-study courses. The previous edition only discussed face-to-face classes and workbooks.

- Most of the chapters describe the design of entirely new training programs under the best possible conditions for practice. But this book acknowledges that in many instances the people designing and developing training programs work under more stringent conditions or on revisions to existing programs. Each chapter includes suggestions for adjusting design practices in these situations.

- Chapter 3 now presents a substantially changed process for analysis, clarified through years of use in the classroom and influenced by changes in the industry practice.

- Chapter 5 now includes more-current suggestions for choosing the format and communication medium of a training program and for structuring the program.

- Chapter 6 now focuses almost exclusively on choosing an instructional strategy, and explains how to formally prepare design plans for review. The information on writing materials for administering activities and opening and closing training programs now appears in chapters 7 and 10.

- Chapter 8 now addresses production for online programs, including slidecasts.

Acknowledgments

This book reflects the influences of many people. First, I would like to thank some of my current and former colleagues and collaborators: Ann-Louise Davidson, for her always fresh and frank perspective on instructional design; Patrick Devey, who worked with me to identify scores of pages of practical issues affecting the design and development of instructional programs; Margaret Driscoll, for engaging in countless conversations about the nature and role of training in the mobile and digital world and for always reminding me about the role of philosophy, theory, and mental models in this work; Louise Grummit, who painstakingly worked through the intricacies of training and instructional design competencies with me; Karen Herland, Barbara

Komorowski, and David Price, all of whom had the courage to edit my teaching practices and, in the process, provided a new and improved perspective on teaching; and Patti Shank, who shares my passion for practice-based research.

Second, I would like to thank the team at the Association for Talent Development (ATD) for more than a decade of patience and support with publishing ventures, conference presentations, workshops, and academic programs. A special shout-out to Justin Brusino, who shepherded this project through the production cycle, and Jack Harlow, who edited the manuscript with a special sensitivity to both its purpose and my hypersensitivity to language. I would also like to thank former ATD staff members, Juana Llorens, who secured the contract for this second edition; and Mark Morrow, who edited the first edition in 2003. I developed a new appreciation for Mark's work when basing this edition on his edited files from the first one.

Most of all, I would like to thank my partner, Marco Manrique, who once again sacrificed evenings and weekends so I could finish another book. Without that quiet understanding and support, I would not have completed this revision.

1

The Basics of Designing Training Programs

 What's Inside This Chapter

This chapter introduces the concept of design for training and provides a foundation of concepts that guide the training process. It addresses:

- What is "design" for training?
- The basic principles that guide course designers: the essential nature of training, humxan performance improvement, and seven "must-follow" principles of adult learning.
- The basic steps involved in designing courses, called ADDIE.

An activity at the end of this chapter helps assess the extent to which you have begun to integrate these foundations into your approach to training.

What Is Design for Training?

A request for training is more than a request for an event or a set of materials. It is a request to help a designated group of workers build a particular set of skills. Learning the skills identified in the request often requires developing related skills and knowledge. And applying those skills on the job often depends on deploying certain motivating factors in the work environment and removing anticipated roadblocks.

To address these challenges, trainers invest substantial effort in designing and developing courses or programs—as many as 40 hours of preparation for each hour of live classroom instruction and up to 12 times that for a self-study course. Before developing a program, trainers spend considerable time defining its goals, identifying the intended learners, and clarifying the context in which learners will use the skills gained in the program. After developing it, trainers test the program to make sure that it is most likely to help learners develop the intended skills.

The framework for clarifying a training problem, defining the intended outcomes, determining how to present the instructional material to learners to achieve those outcomes, developing the training program according to these designs, launching and running—or implementing—the program, and evaluating its effectiveness is called the *instructional design process.* Trainers use the process to prepare all types of programs—those delivered in physical and virtual classrooms, as well as self-study courses like workbooks and online tutorials. Trainers call this process *design* because it solves a problem, and design is fundamentally a problem-solving process.

Basic Principles of Training Design

Training design is guided by certain principles: the essential nature of training; the key principles of human performance improvement; and the must-follow principles of adult learning. The following sections explore each of these principles.

The Essential Nature of Training

With the Internet, people have access to free online courses from Harvard, MIT, and many other universities; museum collections from the Metropolitan Museum of Art, the British Museum, and the Smithsonian Institution; blogs from people all over the world sharing their hard-learned advice; encyclopedic information from Wikipedia; and YouTube videos, ranging from how to tie a tie to how to determine the confidence levels in the statistical analysis of sales data. People are thus surrounded by learning opportunities.

Or are they?

Learning is a more complex activity than merely providing information to people and hoping they figure out what to do with it. Cognitive psychology—the branch of psychology that studies the processes of the brain—studies learning in depth. Cognitive psychologists define learning as a change in behavior and thought, and they determine whether learning occurred by observing if the person who was expected to change behaviors and thought processes—the learner—has actually adopted the designated behaviors and thought processes.

Trainers usually focus on developing complex behaviors and thought processes—or skills—that consist of many contributing behaviors, such as recommending products to prospective customers. For example, to recommend products to a prospective customer, a sales representative must first learn the needs of the customer and then identify several possible products that might address the customer's needs.

Basic Rule 1

The purpose of training is to develop the competencies and skills of learners. Developing competencies and skills involves more than merely distributing information to learners. It involves developing particular behaviors and thought processes and verifying that learners have mastered them.

Sometimes trainers focus on changing physical behaviors, such as following a new process for changing tires on a car, which others can easily observe. These skills are called *psychomotor skills*. Sometimes trainers focus on changing intellectual behaviors and thought processes, such as following a new methodology for determining creditworthiness. These skills are called *cognitive skills*. And sometimes trainers focus on changing attitudes, such as attitudes toward diversity. These skills are called *affective skills*. Although feasible, observing affective skills admittedly poses challenges.

In addition to explaining concepts and describing and demonstrating processes, developing skills also involves providing learners with opportunities to practice skills, receive feedback on their performance, and continue practicing until they master the skills. Similarly, developing skills also includes verifying that learners actually acquired the skills. The availability of practice, feedback, and assessment distinguishes formal training programs from other informational materials that purport to teach.

Three Key Principles of Improving Human Performance

More than merely teaching people to perform tasks and develop skills, training programs are a piece of a larger effort to help organizations develop their staff—or talent—and achieve meaningful goals. These programs help organizations build the competencies of workers and help groups perform their assigned responsibilities so that organizations can achieve their goals most effectively and efficiently.

Human performance improvement (HPI) is a framework that places training and talent development efforts within broader efforts to help organizations achieve their goals. It notes that many people working in a variety of positions help organizations achieve meaningful goals. HPI provides a means for determining the role (if any) that training might play in addressing the issues facing an organization. Three principles of HPI play a profound role in training design.

 Think About This

You might often hear several words used interchangeably to refer to training, but note that each has a precise definition.

- *Training* refers to the development of skills, competencies, and knowledge for immediate use (typically within the next six months). Therefore, training typically focuses on work-related skills.

- *Education* refers to the development of skills, knowledge, and competencies for long-term use. Although some learners might apply their education immediately, instructors also hope that learners retain the material for many years. For example, trainers might provide leadership development programs to those currently in junior positions in hopes of developing a new generation of senior professionals.

- *Learning* refers to an activity performed by the person who receives training or education, and is observed as a change in behavior. Although trainers facilitate learning, only the participants can do the learning.

---

1. Training Programs Must Address Meaningful Goals

   Trainers work with sponsors (the internal or external parties that commission the design of training programs) to establish meaningful goals for the training program. They limit instructional material to that which helps learners achieve the goals. And they determine the success of the program by its ability to achieve the established goals, as well as the larger organizational goals to which the program contributes. If the purpose of the training program is to develop the competence of workers to perform their job, trainers must first define the overall competence desired, next identify the specific skills that contribute to the competence desired, and then devise a means of assessing whether learners have achieved the competence desired.

2. Training Programs Must Address the Gap Between Current and Desired Performance

Many sponsors request training programs because they've observed an issue in their environment, such as difficulties with certain types of sales, errors in the operations of certain services, or inadequate adherence to safety standards. They attribute the issue to a lack of competence and skill on the part of workers, and thus believe that training programs could help resolve the issue.

In other words, they perceive a disparity between current and desired performance—a disparity called the *performance gap*. Although the gap itself is usually self-evident, the reasons that it exists usually are not. The cause of the gap is best uncovered through an analysis of the situation.

3. Training Programs Alone Might Not Fill the Performance Gap

Training might help bridge the performance gap, but sometimes it is not enough. Why? Well, training addresses just one of the three drivers of performance: skills and knowledge. In some instances, workers have the skills and knowledge to perform a task, but still do not perform it effectively.

Training doesn't address the other two drivers of performance: tools and resources (the materials used and processes followed to perform the task) and motivation (the interest in performing the task effectively and efficiently). If the performance gap results from a lack of skills and knowledge, training can address it. But if the performance gap results from a lack of resources, a poorly defined or planned process, or motivational issues, training is not likely to be effective in bridging the performance gap.

 **Basic Rule 2**

Training is a goal-focused activity. For the individuals who participate in it, training can help them build competencies and skills needed to succeed on the job. For the organizations who sponsor it, training can help organizations achieve their goals.

This book explains how to design training courses and exclusively focuses on performance gaps resulting from a lack of skills and knowledge. Despite that singular focus, keep in mind that training might not always be the solution to the issues driving a request for a training program.

Seven Must-Follow Principles of Adult Learning

Adult learners should be taught differently than school children. That's because adults enter training with experience, with preconceived notions about the subject and with needs emerging from their responsibilities as workers, parents, and citizens—characteristics unique to adult learners. So, when designing and presenting training programs, consider the following principles to treat adult learners like adults.

Adult Learning Is Andragogy, Not Pedagogy

Andragogy, a term popularized by Malcolm Knowles, refers to the art and science of teaching adults (Knowles 1973; Knowles, Holton, and Swanson 2011). Andragogy encompasses principles that instructional designers must address when preparing training programs for adults. In contrast, *pedagogy* refers to the art and science of teaching children, whose learning needs differ significantly from those of adults.

Adult Learners Are Pressed for Time

Adults squeeze in learning among demanding jobs, family responsibilities, and community commitments. Even when highly motivated to learn, the call of life limits the time that many adults can invest in learning. In practical terms, this suggests that you should limit the amount of outside-of-class work because learners might not have time to even start it.

Adult Learners Are Goal Oriented

Adults primarily participate in learning programs to achieve a particular goal. In the context of training, the goal is typically work related. The goal might have immediate benefits, such as learning to use a work-related software application. Or the goal might have longer-term implications, such as mastering the essentials of planning projects to become qualified for a project management role. So begin work on training programs by asking how learners can benefit from it.

Adult Learners Bring Previous Knowledge and Experience

Adult learners bring a lifetime of knowledge and experience to each training program. When that knowledge and experience directly relates to the new material in the program, linking the two can create a powerful and relevant learning experience. Learners might already know some or all of the content that the program addresses. To avoid wasting their time, training designers need to carefully assess what learners already know and let them skip familiar material or explain why reviewing the material benefits learners.

In some instances, content in the training program may conflict with previous knowledge and experience, and training designers may thus need to help learners unlearn old behaviors and thought processes so that they can adopt the new ones promoted in the program.

Adult Learners Have a Finite Capacity for Information

Although many training programs tackle complex topics, most learners are primarily interested in aspects of the content that directly affect them, which in many cases is just a small part of the program. But because trainers often have so little time with learners, they try to cram in as much content as they can—to the detriment of learners. In addition, the human brain can only process a limited amount of information at a time, placing some practical limitations on the quantity of material a learner can digest in a program. Design practices advocated by this book—especially establishing objectives (see chapter 4) and adopting the minimalist approach (see chapters 5 and 6)—help designers work within these human limitations.

Adult Learners Go Through Several Phases
When Developing Competence in Their Jobs

During the first six weeks to three months on a job, adults are highly motivated to learn. When faced with a new work process or approach, adults are similarly motivated to learn. (What stifles their motivation, at this point, is fear of failure and difficulty of unlearning old habits, an issue called *self-efficacy.*)

As learners become more competent, motivation to learn wanes unless a specific need arises. The challenge for training designers is identifying the development level of learners as their expertise builds and then adjusting the content to match that level.

True Learning Happens When Adults Successfully
Integrate—or Transfer—the Skills Into Their Daily Routines

Although adults develop new competencies and skills through formal training programs, the only way those new competencies and skills can meaningfully affect their lives is when learners actually apply them. When designing effective training programs, trainers consider not only how training is delivered in the classroom environment but also how it transfers to the job.

 Think About This

Most people go through several stages of motivation and development as they build their competency levels (Carliner 2002):

- *Unaware stage:* At this stage, learners are unfamiliar with the issue addressed by the training program, have little interest in the issue, or both. The challenge at this stage is motivating learners to proceed with the learning process.

- *Novice stage:* At this stage, learners' primary learning goal is getting started—learning enough material to proficiently handle the routine tasks. Learners only need how-to instruction, practice opportunities, and feedback on first attempts at practice at this point. Don't overburden learners with too much material or overwhelm them with unnecessary choices. For example, if teaching learners how to cut and paste text in a word processor, just teach the easiest way to do so, not five ways to do so. Each additional way only confuses learners.

- *Feeling arrogant stage:* At this stage, learners have mastered routine tasks and gained confidence, and now they want to learn how to handle the routine tasks more efficiently as well as less common tasks. Learners still want instruction at this point, but some seek less guidance and practice. So just tell learners what to do; let them choose whether they want to practice.

- *Feeling humble stage:* At this stage, learners have mastered most of the material in their area of expertise and are aware of the limits of their knowledge. Learning usually happens informally, one expert to another. In these situations, learners benefit from models and frameworks for approaching challenges, and appreciate discussion groups and other, less formal learning programs in which they can converse with experts to explore answers to their specific questions.

The ADDIE Approach to Instructional Design

With the principles of HPI and andragogy guiding them, trainers design programs. When creating training programs, training designers and developers follow five broad activities—analysis, design, development, implementation, and evaluation—called ADDIE. The following sections introduce each of these activities.

Basic Rule 3

To best support adult learners in developing new skills and competencies, treat them as individuals. Avoid approaching training as a one-size-fits-all venture. When feasible, adjust training to respond to the individuality of participants.

Analysis

Analysis encompasses the tasks required to clarify the need driving the training request and define the requirements that the training program should achieve.

To clarify the need underlying the request to design and develop a training program, you need to determine what the sponsor of the request hopes to accomplish through the training program—the business need to be addressed and the performance gap to be bridged. You also need to learn about the workers who will participate in the training program—who they are, what they already know, how they feel about their jobs, and the challenges they might experience as they work toward new levels of performance after the program.

In the analysis, you also need to identify any barriers that restrict learners from applying the skills taught in training to their job, as well as more general factors that could affect the design and development of the program, such as the drop-dead due date for the project and the not-to-exceed budget (the maximum the organization sponsoring the training course is willing to invest). Chapter 3 identifies in more detail the information you need to start a training project.

To define the requirements of the training program, you need to write objectives (formal statements of goals) that the program should achieve and prepare evaluations to determine whether learners have achieved those objectives. Writing objectives involves stating the tasks that learners must perform to successfully bridge the performance gap identified earlier. Trainers use specific language to write objectives so that others can assess whether learners have achieved them.

> ### ✓ Basic Rule 4
>
> Effective training programs require a thorough understanding of the training request, a clear statement of the expected results, a well-thought-out plan for achieving the results, and a means of determining whether the training program achieved them. The ADDIE approach guides trainers in doing so, by breaking down the design process into manageable tasks.

You also need to prepare the evaluations that assess whether learners have achieved the objectives. Test questions emerge directly from the objectives and require that learners meaningfully apply the material. You can then design programs in such a way that they "teach to the test" to ensure that largest number of learners master the objectives. Chapter 4 explains how to write effective objectives and tests.

Design

Through design, you determine how to develop the skills identified in the objectives and prepare learners to apply those skills in the ways that the tests assess. Specifically, design involves:

- *Choosing the appropriate intervention for achieving the objectives.* Although this book assumes that training is the appropriate solution to the problem, in the real world, training on its own might not achieve the desired performance. Training only addresses a performance gap that results from a lack of skills and knowledge. Other types of programs—called interventions—address performance gaps from a lack of resources or motivation. As noted earlier, this book focuses on training and does not explore other possible interventions.
- *Choosing the appropriate communication medium.* Course designers and developers can use different communication media to deliver training to leaners, including the physical classroom, the live virtual classroom, workbooks, and computers. The general design activities for these media are similar, though some adjustments might be necessary to take advantage of certain unique capabilities of a medium and avoid its pitfalls. Chapter 5 describes the primary media used to deliver training programs and offers some design considerations for each.
- *Structuring the instructional material for the training program.* Structuring the material involves first determining a sequence for presenting content—that is, what comes first and what comes second. In doing so, you consider the general structure of each unit

so that units have a similar rhythm, divide the content into manageable units, and determine the specific material to cover in each. You also determine whether variations of particular units are needed to address specific groups of learners, such as learners who follow an alternate process when applying the content. Chapter 5 explains how to structure the content.

- *Presenting the instructional material.* After determining the structure of the program, you next choose a strategy for teaching the instructional material. You choose a general strategy for the entire program as well as specific strategies for individual units, such as the classical approach, mastery learning, and discovery learning. As part of choosing a teaching strategy, you also determine the sequence of events needed in each unit to develop the skills identified, such as starting a lesson with an activity or waiting until after an instructor demonstrates a skill before starting an activity. Chapter 6 describes the different techniques available.

Development

Development is when you convert design plans to reality. For classroom-based training programs (whether face-to-face or in the live virtual classroom), you develop lesson plans, slides, lecture notes, handouts, and an instructor guide for administering learning activities. You might also create databases and other materials for computer-based exercises, answer keys for question-and-answer exercises, and discussion guides for class discussions. For self-study programs, you develop workbooks or online tutorials that learners can take with little or minimal assistance from another person, as well as readings and guides for tutors. Chapter 7 identifies the types of materials you must develop for training programs. Chapter 8 describes guidelines for writing and designing these materials and offers some considerations for producing them.

In addition, during development you also make sure that the program will achieve its objectives through three types of reviews. Pilot tests with people who represent the intended learners are used to find out which parts of the program work well and which parts need further work. In technical reviews, SMEs verify the accuracy of the instructional materials. In production reviews, editors or fellow trainers review a program as if they were its first learners. Chapter 9 describes these reviews and explains how to prepare for them.

Implementation

After developing the materials, you make the training program available to the intended learners. To ensure that learners become aware of it, you need to promote the program. You also need to provide ways for learners to enroll in the program and provide the online or classroom facilities for doing so. In addition, you need to track the progress of learners and provide assistance when learners need it. Last, you need to record when learners complete programs and then administer evaluations. This process is called *implementation.*

Although many course designers and developers do not handle many of these tasks, you need to make sure that others properly handle them. Effective implementation is essential to learners mastering the objectives, which in turn helps sponsors achieve the goals established for the training program. Chapter 10 describes the implementation of training programs.

Evaluation

Evaluation involves assessing whether the training program achieved its goals. Goals involve people mastering skills in training and then sustaining that mastery over a long period of time. As a result, evaluation is an ongoing process rather than a one-time event.

Within the training community, the most widely used approach to this ongoing process of evaluation was developed by late University of Wisconsin professor and ATD officer, Donald Kirkpatrick. The Kirkpatrick model (1994) considers the effectiveness of training programs at four levels (Table 1-1).

This book primarily addresses Levels 1 and 2. Chapter 4 presents a sample of a satisfaction survey (Level 1) and describes how to develop a criterion-referenced test (Level 2). Other books in this Training Basics series explain in more detail how to evaluate training programs at all four levels of this model.

Table 1-1. Kirkpatrick's Four Levels of Evaluation

Level	Name	Issues Assessed at This Level
1	Reaction	Assesses learners' initial reactions to a training program immediately after the program. Their reactions, in turn, offer insights into learners' satisfaction with the program. Trainers usually assess satisfaction through a survey, often called a "smile sheet." Occasionally, trainers use focus groups and similar methods to receive descriptive specific comments (called *descriptive* or *qualitative feedback*) on the programs.
2	Learning	Assesses the extent to which learners achieved the objectives established for the program. Trainers usually assess learning with a *criterion-referenced* test conducted immediately following the training program. The criteria are the course objectives. The tests usually involve answering questions or participating in a demonstration observed by an instructor.

| 3 | Transfer | Assesses the extent to which learners actually apply the skills learned in a program in everyday work six weeks to six months or longer after completing the program. This assessment is based on the objectives of the program and carried out through observations, surveys, and interviews with co-workers and supervisors. Some organizations assess transfer several times to determine how well learners sustain the use of the skills on the job. |
| 4 | Business results | Assesses the impact of the training program on the bottom line of the organization six months to two years after the program is completed (the actual time varies depending on the context of the course). |

Source: Kirkpatrick (1994).

Getting It Done

This chapter provides a foundation of knowledge that you can apply when designing and developing training programs. Use Exercise 1-1 to assess your mastery of this foundation and check your responses against the answer key.

Exercise 1-1. Reinforcing the Basic Principles of Design

Fill in the blanks.

1. Design is:

_____

_____

2. Learning is:

_____

_____

3. The purpose of training is:

_____

_____

4. Human performance improvement refers to:

_____

_____

5. The three components of human performance improvement are:

_____

_____

6. Nearly all training is intended for adults, who approach learning differently than children. Name at least three of the seven principles of adult learning described in this chapter.

_____

_____

Exercise 1-1. Reinforcing the Basic Principles of Design (continued)

7. ADDIE is an acronym for the main steps in designing training programs. What does ADDIE stand for?

A _____

D _____

D _____

I _____

E _____

Answers

1. Design is a problem-solving activity and, in terms of training, refers to the framework for analyzing a training problem, defining the intended outcomes, determining how to present the content to learners to achieve those outcomes, developing the training program according to the designs, implementing the program, and evaluating its effectiveness.
2. Learning is a change in behavior and thought. Trainers determine whether learning occurred by observing whether the person who was expected to change behaviors and thought processes—the learner—has actually adopted the designated behaviors and thought processes.
3. The purpose of training is to develop the competencies and skills of learners. Developing competencies and skills involves more than merely distributing information to learners.
4. Human performance improvement (HPI) is a framework that places training and talent development efforts within broader efforts to help organizations achieve their goals. HPI notes that many people working in a variety of positions help organizations achieve meaningful goals.
5. Three principles guide HPI:
   • All training programs must address meaningful goals. Furthermore, these measurable improvements should offer tangible benefits to the organization sponsoring the training program.
   • Training programs must address the gap between current and desired performance.
   • Training programs alone might not fill the performance gap. They only fill gaps caused by a lack of skills and knowledge. Other causes include a lack of appropriate resources and a lack of motivation.
6. The seven principles of adult learning are:
   • Adult learning is andragogy, not pedagogy.
   • Adult learners are pressed for time.
   • Adult learners are goal oriented.
   • Adult learners bring previous knowledge and experience.
   • Adult learners have a finite capacity for information.
   • Adult learners go through several phases when developing competence in their jobs.
   • True learning happens when adults successfully integrate—or transfer—the skills into their daily routines.
7. ADDIE is an acronym that stands for analysis, design, development, implementation, and evaluation. Specifically, ADDIE involves:
   • Analysis, which refers to the activities performed for clarifying the training problem and defining the objectives the training course should achieve. Analysis involves researching the problem, defining the objectives, and preparing the assessment.
   • Design, through which trainers determine how to present that content. Specifically, design involves choosing the appropriate intervention for achieving the objectives, choosing the communication method to deliver the content (such as a classroom or online), structuring the instructional materials, and choosing an instructional strategy for teaching the material.
   • Development, through which trainers convert design plans into program materials. Specifically, development involves preparing program materials and then testing and reproducing them.
   • Implementation, through which you bring the program to learners. Implementation involves scheduling courses, arranging for ongoing support of learners, and marketing and maintaining courses.
   • Evaluation, which assesses whether the training programs have achieved their objectives. Evaluation occurs at these four levels: (1) reaction, (2) learning, (3) transfer, and (4) business impact.

2

The Basics of Planning a Training Project

 What's Inside This Chapter

This chapter introduces the basics of planning the schedule and budget for a training project. Specifically, this chapter addresses:

- Who needs to be a part of a training project team and what each team member contributes to the project
- Which issues to address when planning a schedule for a training project
- How to realistically estimate the cost of a project.
- How to determine the scope of your project—the extent of effort you plan to invest in the project.

The worksheets at the end of this chapter can help you apply this information to plan a project.

Getting Started

Because training projects happen within the workplace before you begin designing and developing a training program, you need to address four business questions likely to arise during the project:

- Who will work on the training program?
- What assumptions underlie the schedule and budget?
- When will the program be completed?
- How much will the program cost?

Who Will Work on the Training Program?

Although as designer and developer you have primary responsibility for developing training programs, many other people play a role in the effort. Each has a different concern about the project. For example, you might encounter a senior vice president anxiously anticipating a training course on a new management policy, a graphic designer waiting for a draft of the content to begin preparing slides, and a project manager waiting to learn the number of hours spent on the project to ensure that you have not gone over budget.

In other words, although your work might often feel solitary, designing and developing effective training programs involves collaborating with many professionals. One of your challenges is figuring out whom to consult, when, and how to blend the different people and their roles into an effective work team.

Project participants fall into two categories: members of the sponsoring organization and members of the training organization. The following sections describe each category of roles, identify the specific roles that people play, and offer suggestions for building an effective work team.

Roles Within the Sponsoring Organization

Whether working in an internal training department or for an external provider of training and instructional design services, most trainers work in a client-like relationship. That is, someone outside of the training organization usually requests that you design and develop a training program that meets the needs of that client. In this book, the client is called the *sponsor*. Within the sponsor's organization, several people take active roles in a training project.

Executive sponsor (also called the benefactor *or* paying client*):* The most senior person who is ultimately responsible for the project. Although you won't have much contact with this person, recognize that because she is the one who can either authorize or stop payment for the project, this executive sponsor is the one who must be satisfied with the results.

Ombudsperson: The person within the sponsor organization from whom you receive managerial direction and who acts as the go-between in the sponsor organization when you need assistance. For example, the ombudsperson might coordinate the reviews of draft training materials and might also recruit learners for a pilot class of a training program. The ombudsperson serves as the official representative of the executive sponsor.

Subject matter experts (SMEs): One or more people who developed the technical content to be addressed by the training program and can attest to its accuracy. Your project may have one or more SMEs, depending on the type of training project and the size of your organization. See Table 2-1 for information about the expertise of SMEs involved in particular types of training projects.

Table 2-1. Training and SMEs

Type of Training	Typical SMEs
Product training	Engineers, programmers, and scientists who designed and developed the product. In many organizations, marketing professionals who have played a role in developing and marketing the product also serve as SMEs.
Marketing training	Marketing managers and staff—that is, people who develop sales strategies, create promotional programs, and oversee the salespeople in the field. In some cases, you might also consult with sales representatives in the field.
Management development	Members of the HR staff and other managers who have responsibility for overseeing company policies, employee supervision, and succession planning.
Medical training (usually pharmaceuticals and medical devices)	Medical staff, engineers, and others involved in the product or service. For regulated products and services, members of the government regulation agency, such as the U.S. Food and Drug Administration, might also serve as an external SME.
New employee orientation	Members of the HR staff and managers from areas addressed in the training.
Manufacturing training	Engineers who designed the manufacturing process and managers of the manufacturing lines affected.

SMEs usually focus on the completeness and accuracy of the content in the training program. They are concerned that you precisely report information. So a misused word will raise concerns. Many SMEs request that you include more information than learners need; however, the superfluous information could end up distracting learners from successfully completing the objectives of the program. In such instances, you need to exercise your judgment about which information benefits learners and which does not, and then diplomatically advocate to SMEs for the needs of the learners when explaining why the material is unnecessary.

Legal staff: A representative from the legal department of the sponsor's organization who verifies the accuracy of actual or implied promises and warranties in the program, checks for the proper use of intellectual property (such as trade or company secrets and material copyrighted by other organizations), and ensures that tests are fair for all learners.

Learners: The people who take the training program. You precisely identify the learners when analyzing the needs for the program (see chapter 3 for more details). Learners primarily focus on the general need for the program and usefulness of its content to their work. Some of the issues that learners consider as they go through a training program are:

- Was the content easy to understand? Did they have all the information they needed to understand a concept or did they have to ask follow-up questions? Did they have to review it several times before understanding?
- Was the information complete? Was something left out?
- Was the information relevant? Could they figure out how to apply it to their jobs?
- Could they perform the skills taught when they returned to the job? Did application of the material in the workplace differ from its presentation in the program?
- How satisfied were they with the training experience? If dissatisfied, what specifically concerned them?

The sponsor's representatives might each serve just one role or one person might serve several. The level of involvement also varies, depending on the combination of roles that sponsor's representatives play, other responsibilities they have, and their interest in the project. Some play a central role in a project; others only play a role on paper.

Roles Within the Training Organization

The process of designing and developing training programs requires the skills of a variety of specialists. Here are the most common roles:

- *Manager:* The person within the organization for whom you work, who has overall responsibility for a project, and reviews your performance on the sponsor's project after its completion.
- *Learning consultant* (also called a relationship manager): The person on the training team who serves as the primary contact with the client organization.
- *Curriculum planner:* The person who plans all of the training in a particular subject area, who determines which programs to include, the content that each program covers, related materials and resources needed to develop this content, and who oversees the evaluation of programs.

- *Course designer and developer:* The person who conducts the analysis of the training need of the training need; chooses and sequences content; drafts training materials such as slides, instructor's notes, and workbooks; and oversees production of the materials.
- *Instructor:* The person who teaches the program and serves as the face of the program to learners.
- *Production specialists:* The people who help develop particular aspects of the training program, and prepare training materials for duplication. The production skills needed for a program vary depending on the communication medium used to deliver the program. Table 2-2 lists the production skills needed for programs in different media.
- *Training administrator:* The person who oversees the running of training programs, including promotional activities, scheduling of classrooms and instructors, enrollment, attention to learners during a class session, recording of programs completed by learners, and compilation of evaluations.

 Basic Rule 5

You work for the sponsor. Without the sponsor, you would have no work, so one of your chief jobs is pleasing the sponsor while remaining an advocate for the learner. That position presents some challenges because the needs of learners and the sponsor sometimes seem at odds. When that happens, remember that the executive sponsor is only able to achieve his or her goals if learners master the training material. Ultimately, the two groups need one another.

On some projects, different people assume these different roles, letting each focus on his or her area of expertise. On the typical project, however, one person assumes several roles. For example, the course designer and developer might also handle all of the production responsibilities for a training program. Note, too, that team members usually work on several projects simultaneously. As a result, people might not be available to work on your project when you need them. The sooner you can anticipate when you need the services of different team members, the better they can arrange their schedule to work when needed.

Table 2-2. Specialized Skills of Production Personnel

Delivery Medium	Production Skills Needed
All training programs	Graphic design and illustration skills, which involve designing the physical appearance of the training materials and preparing artwork and similar images, such as medical illustrations and drawings of new products. (People often confuse illustrators and graphic designers. Illustrators draw things; graphic designers plan the overall appearance of text and illustrations.)
Live virtual classroom (webcasts or webinars)	Webcast production, which involves coordinating the live presentation of webcasts, coaching presenters on the technology and presentation skills in advance and during the program (especially presenters with little or no experience), and addressing technical issues that might arise during the webcast.
Self-study online materials	Authoring and programming skills. Authoring involves using specialized software called authoring systems to prepare information for presentation online. Programing involves writing computer instructions. Training projects need programming to address situations in which authoring systems cannot present material as the course designer and developer planned. A programmer writes the missing instructions for the computer.
Video presentations	Video production skills, which include setting up and recording video sequences (which involve setting up recording in a workplace so that ambient sound is minimized), sound and video editing (the process of taking various clips or scenes, usually shot out of order, and assembling them into a single file), acting and narration, and directing.
Audio presentations	Sound production skills, which include narration and sound editing (compiling recordings made at separate times into a cohesive whole).
Printed materials	Desktop publishing skills, which involve using software and hardware designated by the organization to produce a master copy of the materials, from which copies will be made.

Building an Effective Work Team

Teamwork is more than sharing labor; it's sharing work. By following certain strategies at the beginning of a project, you increase the likelihood that the team will work together cohesively throughout the project. Here are some issues to address at the beginning of a project to ensure that it flows smoothly as possible.

Decision-making: How does the group make a decision? By consensus? By majority vote? Does the leader decide? Before making the first decision, determine as a team how you will make decisions. By openly discussing the decision-making process in your first meeting, you can avoid problems later. For example, if you have decided that all major decisions are to be made by consensus, team members know that they should not be making unilateral decisions that affect the entire project, such as the format of all screens in an online training program.

Conflict resolution: What happens if the group can't reach consensus on a decision? Do you not make a decision, defer to someone's judgment, or take a vote? And what happens if two people can't work together? Does someone intervene? Do you let them work out the conflict by themselves?

Often, teams tend to avoid conflict and the unresolved issues rip apart their fabric. The people at the center of the fray often try to recruit other team members to their side. Instead of a cohesive unit, the team becomes warring factions. Deciding how to handle conflict before you actually experience it gives you a strategy for dealing with conflict should it arise.

Noted

The training professionals on a project, especially the learning consultant, project manager, curriculum planner, and course designer and developer, might have a credential, such as the ATD's Certified Professional in Learning and Performance. Such credentials validate the competence of the training professional and represent a commitment to the field.

Individual commitment expected: Like most aspects of team work, each team member has a different concept of commitment. Some believe that commitment means devoting 24 hours a day to a project. Others believe that commitment means full attention during work hours only. Still others believe that commitment involves weekend and late night work at some times, but not for an indefinite stretch. Others have family commitments that make them unavailable outside work hours. Discuss the degree of commitment that you expect from each team member to gain a shared set of expectations.

Relationship building: After starting a project, take time to get to know one another and become comfortable working together. Until reaching that comfort level, be on your best behavior in the first few team meetings until you become accustomed to working together.

Planning the Project

In addition to establishing a project team, starting a training project begins with preparing the schedule and budget. The following sections describe assumptions that you should first identify and then offer simple methods for preparing a proposed schedule and budget.

What Assumptions Underlie the Schedule and Budget?

Before planning the schedule and budget, first identify and explicitly state the assumptions on which you are basing these plans. Doing so can help you manage the sponsor's expectations and ensure that the sponsor is satisfied.

 Basic Rule 6

Before you make a commitment to complete a training program within a certain schedule and budget, explicitly state the assumptions on which you make those promises and share them with your sponsor. The schedule and budget for a successful project emerge from those assumptions. If these assumptions change later or prove incorrect, you can work with your sponsor to renegotiate the schedule and budget.

Several issues affect the estimates of training projects. The first two issues are the *drop-dead deadline* and the *not-to-exceed cost*. The drop-dead deadline refers to the date when the sponsor must have the program to make it available to learners. Most training programs support a related business activity, such as the launch of a new product, process, or policy. The sponsor must train learners when that launch begins; receiving the program a week late reflects disastrously on the sponsor.

The not-to-exceed cost refers to the maximum amount the sponsor can afford to spend on the training program. This, in turn, suggests whether you can afford certain options for your program, such as costly video and face-to-face instruction.

If the sponsor does not voluntarily share the drop-dead deadline and not-to-exceed cost, try as best as possible to press them to do so, or to explicitly say that no such deadline or cost limit exists. Doing so clarifies expectations.

The third issue likely to affect the estimate is the stability of subject matter. For example, the process for solving 2 + 2 is well established and not likely to change while you develop a training program on simple addition. In contrast, a new tax law is likely to undergo several changes as it works its way through the legislative process; if you develop related training while the legislature debates the law, the training will need to change each time the legislation changes.

The less stable the subject matter, the more likely that you will need to completely revise sections that you have already designed and developed. By accounting for this instability in your planning, you help make your sponsor aware of the potential impact of changes. Focus on these issues:

- Identify, as specifically as possible, the aspects of the subject matter that are not stable.
- State what is not stable about the subject matter.
- Identify the sections affected by the unstable subject matter.
- Determine how to respond to the instability.

For example, you might double or triple your estimates of the schedule to provide suitable time to respond to unanticipated changes. Or you might put conditions on the sponsor, stating that you must have certain issues resolved by certain dates or you reserve the right to miss the proposed schedule.

The fourth issue likely to affect the estimate is the material that you do not intend to cover. Explicitly state what you plan to include in the program—and what you will omit. Although this should have been obvious from the design plans for the program, the sponsor might have only noticed what you included, not what you excluded, and might ask you to insert it after you have completed a draft of the program, adding time and cost to the project.

By explicitly stating what you do not intend to cover, the sponsor is made aware of the program's limitations. If the sponsor is not comfortable with the content being excluded, you can revise your design plans and, as a result, the schedules and budgets. Or if your sponsor later asks you to add some of the material that you excluded, you have a basis for renegotiating the budget and schedule.

When Will the Program Be Completed?

Designing a training program is a complex effort, bringing together different pieces—such as the slides, instructor guide, and student materials—that you might develop separately. In addition you must have some assurance that the materials really work. For these reasons, development of a training program involves a series of intermediate steps called *milestones* or *checkpoints* so that the project is handled in manageable parts.

Basic Rule 7

Setting the proposed schedule involves estimating the size of the project, estimating the total length of the project in workdays, and establishing intermediate deadlines.

Estimate the Size of the Project

When assigned to work on training programs to be taught in the live or virtual (webinar) classroom, many sponsors and project managers also tell you the intended length of the program, such as a half-day, one day, two days, or one week. When planning such a project, begin by assuming that the length of the program is accurate. (Be sure to make note of this assumption, however.) If you find that you have too much or too little material for the intended length, you might suggest a change in length after you plan the project.

When designing e-learning and workbooks, you are often expected to estimate the length of a project in total number of screens or pages. Experienced course designers and developers can suggest a length, based on the length of similar projects they have designed and developed in the past. If you do not have experience, however, the best time to estimate the length of a project is after you have prepared the design for the training program. At that point, you have an idea of exactly what content will be included, how you will present it, and how many screens or pages you need to present the material.

Unfortunately, most sponsors would like an estimate of the project schedule before you prepare the designs. In those instances, you must take your best guess. Then, you add a fudge factor to account for any uncertainty. Use the fudge factor to increase the size of your project. The fudge factor can vary, depending on a variety of conditions (Table 2-3).

Table 2-3. Fudge Factors for Training Projects

If You Are Dealing With	Add the Following Amount of Time to Your Schedule as a Fudge Factor:
Extremely stable subject matter	10–20 percent
Somewhat stable subject matter	20–30 percent
Unstable subject matter or an unreliable sponsor	As much as 50–100 percent

Consider this example: Your sponsor has asked you to develop a short training program about a new policy that the sponsor estimates will last one hour. You assess that the subject matter is unstable. The sponsor has even acknowledged some aspects of the policy could change up until the last minute. According to Table 2-3, you should add a 50–100 percent fudge factor:

To compute the 50 percent fudge factor:

1 hour × 0.50 (fudge factor) = 0.5 hours

Add the fudge factor to the screen estimate:

1 hour + 0.5 hours = 1.5 hours

Therefore, the estimated number length of the training program, including the fudge factor, is 1.5 hours.

Estimate the Total Length of the Project in Workdays

After estimating the size of the project, next determine the total number of workdays needed for the project. Note that a workday is not the same as a regular day. Although a week contains seven days, it only contains five workdays. In this step, you calculate the total number of workdays needed to complete the project. This calculation will vary depending on whether you are setting the deadline or the sponsor is.

When You Set the Deadline. This is the ideal situation. You can establish the final deadline for the project based on the amount of time really needed to complete the project.

To compute the total number of workdays needed, you use an estimate that varies depending on the medium of instruction, such as a face-to-face classroom course or a basic self-study e-learning program. Research by Bryan Chapman (2010) and Karl Kapp and Robyn Defelice (2009) provides some. Until you have experience, these estimates provide a realistic basis for setting the schedule.

- Workbook-based courses: 4–6 hours of work for every finished page in the workbook.
- Face-to-face classroom courses: 25–40 hours of work for every finished hour of instruction.
- Live virtual courses (webinars): 40–80 hours of work for every finished hour of instruction—40 for an experienced team; 80 for a less-experienced team.
- Basic self-study e-learning courses (recorded narration, slide presentations, quizzes): 79 hours of work for every finished hour of instruction.
- Moderately interactive self-study e-learning courses (custom designed and developed, some interactive sections, brief video sequences): 180–220 hours of work for every finished hour of instruction.
- Highly interactive self-study e-learning courses (extensive video sequences, highly engaging simulations and games, other unique features): 450 hours of work for every finished hour of instruction.

The fundamental concept underlying these estimates is the concept of "finished hour on instruction." A finished hour of instruction represents all the work involved in preparing the instruction: review time, management time, editing time, and preparation of graphics—not just the time of the course designer and developer. In addition, these estimates include the time needed to prepare student materials used in the course.

Figure 2-1 shows an example for calculating the time necessary to complete a classroom training program.

Figure 2-1. Calculating the Total Time Needed to Develop a Classroom Training Program

Rate (25–40 hours of work for every completed hour of instruction) × number of hours

Assume that the training program lasts 1.5 days. Also assume that one day of instruction results in 6.5 hours of actual contact time in the classroom (the rest of the eight hours is spent on breaks). Therefore, the actual length of the training program in hours is:

1.5 × 6.5 = 9.75 hours of instruction

Because the course designer and developer has some familiarity with the content, assume that work progresses at a rate of 35 hours of work for a finished hour of instruction (slightly faster than the 40 hours recommended).

9.75 hours of instruction	×	35 hours of work per finished hour of instruction	=	341.25 hours of completed work (represents contributions by everyone on the team)

How many work weeks are involved? To get the basic number of workweeks, divide the total number of hours—in this case 341.25—into five-day workweeks: just under 8.6 weeks.

But you have not yet considered time away for holidays, sick leave, and other purposes. Add 20 percent to your estimate to arrive at the total number of work weeks needed to complete the project:

(8.6 × 0.2) + 8.6 = 10.32 weeks

The total number of weeks estimated for this project is 10.32 weeks.

When Your Sponsor Has an Inflexible Final Deadline. When sponsors approach you to develop a training program, they often have an inflexible final deadline when they need the finished program—the drop-dead deadline. When the sponsor has such a deadline, develop the schedule so that you can provide the program to sponsors on the date requested.

All the same, compute the total time needed to complete the project as you would using the previous method. Although you might not have all of this time available to design and develop your training program, you might be able to use this information to request assistance in completing the project, such as a second designer and developer.

Consider the example in Figure 2-1. You have estimated that the project will take 10.3 weeks, but the sponsor needs it in eight weeks. By making the sponsor aware that you have removed 2.3 weeks from the schedule (about 25 percent of the total time of the project), you might need additional people or resources to compensate for the lost time.

Establish Intermediate Deadlines

The calculation in Figure 2-1 indicated the *total* time needed to develop the training program. This time includes not only the time needed for drafting the program, but also for conducting the analysis, copying and distributing review drafts, conducting a trial run of the program, and producing the materials. The time includes not just your time, but also the time invested by others, such as SMEs who review the program, the graphic designer who produces the slides, and the production assistants who help produce and duplicate the materials.

Your next challenge is to identify the intermediate deadlines so that each person has sufficient time to do his or her job. These intermediate deadlines are called *milestones*. The phases in the process described in chapter 1 represent most of the milestones, but additional milestones are included because they alert various people involved in developing a training program when you need their assistance.

The amount of time assigned to each step is a percentage of time of the total project (Hackos 1994). To assign intermediate deadlines, then, you would divide the time between now and the final deadline into four main chunks. Table 2-4 provides a worked example for estimating the time needed for intermediate deadlines, assuming you have 11 weeks to design and develop the course.

Table 2-4. Estimating Intermediate Deadlines for a Training Design Project and Assigning Dates

Milestone	Percentage of Total Project	Length of Time Needed	Dates (Assumes a Start Date of September 1)
Analysis: Although you do not separately schedule these activities (you just schedule a single analysis), leave time for: • Conducting research • Interviewing • Reporting the needs analysis • Approving the report • Writing objectives • Preparing an evaluation plan • Receiving informal approval for the objectives and evaluation plan	10–15 percent of the total project length	1 week	September 8

(continued)

Table 2-4. Estimating Intermediate Deadlines for a Training Design Project and Assigning Dates (continued)

Milestone	Percentage of Total Project	Length of Time Needed	Dates (Assumes a Start Date of September 1)
Design: Although you only schedule time for a draft of the design, a review, and a revision, leave time for: • Choosing form and medium • Structuring content • Preparing design plans • Reviewing and revising the design plans with the sponsor and potential learners • Preparing production guidelines (editorial, technical, production, and usability guidelines) • Getting final approval for the project plan	15–20 percent	2 weeks	September 22
First draft	25 percent	2.5 weeks	October 6
First review by SMEs and peers in your organization: Be realistic with review time; people cannot review 600 slides in a day or two. Also, make sure that you leave time for copying (if distributing printed review copies) and mailing (to and from you) as well as time for meetings to clarify review comments	Part of the total time of developing the first draft, but you need to inform reviewers when copies are going to be sent	Set aside 3 days of the 2 weeks spent developing the first draft	October 9
Second draft	15 percent	1.5 weeks	October 16
Second review	Part of the total time of developing the second draft	Set aside 2 days of the 1.5 weeks	October 20
Third draft (optional)	10 percent	1 week	October 24
Third review (optional)	Part of the total time of developing the third draft	Set aside 1 day of the 1 week	October 27
Final draft	5 percent	0.5 week	October 30
Production: Although you do not separately schedule these activities, leave time for: • Copyediting • Preparing materials for duplication or printing • Testing materials (especially needed for online materials, in which unexpected programming errors might arise) • Printing	10 percent	1.5 weeks	November 9
Shipping and distribution of materials	5–10 percent	1 week (up to 4 weeks, depending on publishing method)	November 16

When assigning specific dates to each activity, make sure that the schedule includes formally scheduled dates for reviews, during which SMEs and others review the draft materials and provide feedback. By formally scheduling reviews, SMEs and other team members can block off time on their own calendars to complete this work and return feedback when you need it.

When scheduling reviews, note that most organizations conduct reviews online. Some organizations use email; others use content management systems to manage the review process. Regardless of the system, make sure that you leave time for the system to deliver the files to reviewers and that you notify reviewers that they can begin the reviews. Systems do not always conduct notifications at the moment you send them.

In some instances, organizations might conduct reviews with printed materials. If you work in such a situation, make sure that you leave sufficient time to copy the draft (at least two days, even with quick-copy services) and send it to reviewers (at least another two days, even with expedited mailing) and for reviewers to return the draft to you (at least another two days). (A tight schedule like the example in Table 2-4 leaves little time for these activities—hence a preference for online reviews.)

As you assign dates to the milestones, note that there's a certain amount of flexibility; the estimating formulas are just that—for estimating.

After completing the proposed schedule, review it with your sponsor to make sure that the sponsor is comfortable with it. Ask the sponsor for a signed commitment to complete all reviews as scheduled. This commitment is necessary because your schedule depends on members of the sponsoring organization completing reviews on schedule. If the sponsor does not meet a scheduled review date, ask for a written commitment that you have the right to delay the project one workday for each workday the reviews are delayed.

Once you have a committed schedule, publish it and make sure that everyone on the project team is aware of it. Regularly remind team members of upcoming deadlines so that you have the assistance needed, when you need it.

How Much Will the Program Cost?

A budget is an itemized estimate of the cost of designing, developing, and producing the training program. Because the most significant cost of the project is labor, and you pay for labor by the amount of time used, much of the budget is based on the length of the project, which you determine when you estimate the schedule.

When estimating labor costs, use the fully burdened cost of team members, such as the course designer and developer, project manager, and production staff. The fully burdened cost not only includes salaries, but also benefits, employment taxes, and

Basic Rule 8

Set the budget after setting the schedule.

related overhead expenses (office space, equipment costs like telephones and computers, and support services like HR).

In addition to labor, consider costs for special project-related equipment (such as a high-definition video camera), software (such as an authoring system), training (such as background training on a new technique or technology used in the program), duplication of materials, and specialized services (such as an outside consultant). Different organizations use different methods for computing these costs. For example, some organizations have an hourly rate that they charge for a course designer and developer that also includes the costs of the project manager. Others separately charge for these services.

Think About This

When preparing a budget, also prepare for problems to arise either during the budgeting process or after the sponsor approves the budget. These potential problems include:

- *Unanticipated costs:* Costs that arise for which you did not plan, such as permission fees for using illustrations and graphics in a training program that were not produced by your staff. Most course designers and developers usually forget to budget for these.

- *Underestimated costs:* Actual costs that exceed estimated costs by more than 3 percent. For example, when estimating the budget, you assumed that you need 450 copies of the student materials but you actually needed 925. You underestimated the cost of copies you'd need.

- *Scope creep:* A situation in which a project involves more work than anticipated when you estimated the budget and schedule. Because the additional scope of work creeps up (usually, a bit at a time), it is called scope creep. Scope creep results either from failing to understand the actual scope of work required by the project or by making incorrect assumptions.

- Some ways to address these problems are:

- *Fudge factors (also called a* contingency): An additional percentage built into a project to give you additional funding should unanticipated problems arise. See the discussion of fudge factors earlier in the chapter for more details.

- *Tracking:* Following how closely schedules and budgets match their estimates. By doing so, you can notify sponsors early if you notice problems arising and negotiate for additional time and budget or, in the case of scope creep, return the project to its original scope.

Table 2-5 shows an example estimate for designing and developing the training program whose schedule was estimated in Figure 2-1. Note that the estimated budget in this example only covers the cost of designing and developing the program, and duplicating materials. It does not include the cost of delivering the program, which would include instructor time and travel, classroom rental, refreshments, administrative assistance, and time learners spend away from work. Furthermore, this estimated budget does not include the cost of reviewers' time except for specialists whom you might contract.

When you have developed your budget, review it with the sponsor. Once you have your sponsor's approval, you can use the budget as a basis for spending on this project.

Table 2-5. Budget Calculation

Budget Item	Time and Rate	Total
Fully "burdened" cost of course designer and developer, 90–100 percent of the total time of the project	10.3 weeks at $85 per hour	$35,020
Fully burdened cost of the project manager, about 15 percent of the total time of the project	1.5 weeks at $100 per hour	$6,180
Fully burdened cost of the production staff, about 15 percent of the total time of the project	1.5 weeks at $100 per hour	$6,180
Costs of specialized services, such as the cost of conducting a usability test	Guestimate	$10,000
Equipment costs, such as the purchase or lease of a special computer for the project	None on this project	0
Software costs, such as the purchase or lease of an authoring system or graphics software	None on this project	0
Training costs associated with the project	One 1-week class out of town	$3,800 ($2,000 for tuition, $1,800 in travel expenses)
Copying and distribution costs for review drafts	Will be handled electronically	0
Production costs, such as the cost of preparing special printing plates	Special setup for cover of the student materials	$1,000
Duplicating costs for the final product, which your printer can provide.	100 pages at $.07 per page, $2 per copy for covers and binding, 450 copies	$4,050
Total		$66,230

Platinum, Silver, and Bronze Types of Projects

The discussion in this chapter assumes that you need to develop an entirely new training program. But designing and developing training programs is not a one-size-fits-all endeavor.

For example, many new programs require less effort than described here. Furthermore, rather than developing an entirely new program, many training projects merely involve revising an existing program. E-learning entrepreneur Elliot Masie (2005) proposed that organizations categorize e-learning projects into one of three tiers of effort. Trainers can thus adjust the level of effort to the tier of the project:

- *Platinum:* the most complex training programs, ones with both a high impact on the organization and a large volume of learners (1,000 or more). Platinum projects thus receive a significant investment of resources from the sponsor. Typical platinum projects include new product training and programs that help sponsors institute major changes organization-wide.

- *Silver:* moderately complex training programs, ones with either a high impact on the organization or a large volume of learners, but not both. Silver projects receive a moderate investment of resources from the sponsor. Typical silver projects include developing technical training programs or compliance training, making major revisions to existing programs (changing most parts of the program or adding new units), and converting ongoing classroom training programs to online formats.

- *Bronze:* the least complex training programs, ones that are simple in scope and require the least design effort. Bronze projects have a limited impact on the organization, have a limited number of learners (fewer than 100), or are determined for other reasons to require limited design effort. Typical bronze projects include revisions to existing programs that only require simple updates to the technical content rather than a wholesale redesign of content, programs whose primary purpose is to document existing processes that are used by a limited number of employees (such as the manufacturing processes used in a single plant by one or two teams, and for whom access to SMEs is easy), and programs compiled from noteworthy, one-time presentations by SMEs that the organization wants to make available on a "just-in-case" basis—that is, just in case someone would like to view the presentation, but without the expectation that large numbers of learners would do so.

Most chapters in this book describe the platinum process—that is, the most thorough version of the process described in a given chapter. A section at the end of each chapter suggests how to adapt the platinum process to silver and bronze projects.

Getting It Done

This section contains four exercises that you can perform to begin planning a training project on which you are currently working: staffing a project, identifying the assumptions underlying the project, estimating the schedule, and estimating the budget.

Exercise 2-1. Staffing a Project

Identify the people within and outside your organization who could serve on the team for your training project.

Roles within the sponsoring organization	Executive sponsor	_____
	Ombudsperson	_____
	SMEs	_____
	Legal	_____
	Learners	_____
Roles within the training organization	Manager	_____
	Learning consultant	_____
	Curriculum planner	_____
	Course designer and developer	_____
	Instructor	_____
	Production specialists	_____
Considerations	Do people play one or more roles?	_____
	Availability of staff when needed?	_____
	Other projects to which staff are assigned?	_____
	How well do the skills and abilities of people proposed for roles match the skills and abilities really needed in those roles?	_____

Exercise 2-2. Identifying Assumptions

Identify the assumptions underlying a project to design and develop a training program.

What does the training program cover?	
What doesn't the training program cover?	
Drop-dead deadline	_____ ____, _____ (month) (day) (year)
Not-to-exceed budget	$_____
Stability of the content	❑ Extremely stable (add 10–20 percent to scheduling estimates) ❑ Somewhat stable subject matter (add 20–30 percent to scheduling estimates) ❑ Unstable subject matter or unreliable sponsor (add 50–100 percent to scheduling estimates)

Exercise 2-3. Estimating the Schedule

Use your knowledge of the project deadline (whether set by you or by the sponsor) to estimate the schedule of a project. Note that to meet the project deadline, several people might need to work together to perform the tasks listed. This exercise assumes a silver or platinum project; bronze projects might involve fewer drafts and reviews, as well as a reduced effort on analysis. This exercise also assumes a one-step-at-a-time approach to managing the project.

Milestone	Percentage of Total Project	Length of Time Needed	Date
Analysis: Although you do not separately schedule these activities (you just schedule a single analysis), leave time for: • Conducting research • Interviewing • Reporting the needs analysis • Approving the report • Writing objectives • Preparing an evaluation plan • Receiving informal approval for the objectives and evaluation plan	10–15 percent of the total project length		

Exercise 2-3. Estimating the Schedule (continued)

Milestone	Percentage of Total Project	Length of Time Needed	Date
Design: Although you will only schedule time for a draft of the design, a review, and a revision, leave time for: • Choosing form and medium • Structuring content • Preparing design plans • Reviewing and revising the design plans with the sponsor and potential learners • Preparing production guidelines (editorial, technical, production, and usability guidelines) • Getting final approval for the project plan	15–20 percent		
First draft	25 percent		
First review by SMEs and peers in your organization: Be realistic with review time; people cannot review 600 slides in a day or two. Also, make sure that you leave time for copying (if distributing printed review copies) and mailing (to and from you) as well as time for meetings to clarify review comments.	Part of the total time of developing the first draft, but you need to inform reviewers when copies are going to be sent		
Second draft	15 percent		
Second review	Part of the total time of developing the second draft		
Third draft (optional)	10 percent		
Third review (optional)	Part of the total time of developing the third draft		
Final draft	5 percent		
Production: Although you do not separately schedule these activities, leave time for: • Copyediting • Preparing materials for duplication or printing • Testing materials (especially needed for online materials, in which unexpected programming errors might arise) • Printing	10 percent		
Shipping and distribution of materials	5–10 percent		

Exercise 2-4. Estimating the Budget

Use your knowledge of the project schedule and not-to-exceed cost to estimate the budget of a project. As you do so, consider unanticipated and underestimated costs, and scope creep, which can result from a failure to understand the extent of work, wrong assumptions, and incomplete information. To compensate for all of these, include fudge factors in the estimates.

Budget Item	Time and Rate (number of hours and rate per hour)	Total Cost
Fully burdened cost of course designer and developer, about 90–100 percent of the total time of the project		
Fully burdened cost of the project manager, about 15 percent of the total time of the project		
Fully burdened cost of the production staff, about 15 percent of the total time of the project		
Costs of specialized services, such as the cost of conducting a usability test		
Equipment costs, such as the purchase or lease of a special computer for the project		
Software costs, such as the purchase or lease of an authoring system or graphics software		
Training costs associated with the project		
Copying and distribution costs for review drafts		
Production costs, such as the cost of preparing special printing plates		
Duplicating costs for the final product, which your printer can provide		
Total		

3

The Basic Information Needed to Start a Project

 ## What's Inside This Chapter

Because training should guide the identified learners in developing the intended skills, designing a training program starts with gathering and interpreting information about these and related issues. This gathering and interpreting of information makes up the analysis phase of instruction.

This chapter explores the first part of the analysis process, specifically:

- The eight basic issues that a needs analysis should address
- The four methods of uncovering needs.

An exercise at the end of this chapter can help you apply this information by structuring the information-gathering process for a project on which you are working.

Eight Types of Information Needed in Training Needs Analysis

When new course designers and developers first start a project, many immediately rush to work on slides, quizzes, student workbooks, and similar materials. After all, sponsors often provide course designers and developers with the particulars: the audience, the material that the program needs to cover, and the date by when you need to complete the project. Therefore, work on the training program can commence. Right?

Wrong.

Although sponsors provide you with information about the program, it might not be complete enough for your purposes. It might even be incorrect. For example, information from the sponsors often overlooks many characteristics about learners and how they might apply the instructional material in their jobs.

 Basic Rule 9

Always begin a training project by conducting an analysis. Even if the sponsor believes that the information already provided to you is complete, verify that information; the sponsor probably collected it for purposes other than training. Also plan to collect additional information that the sponsor did not to gain a complete picture of the intended learners, how they plan to use the content, and other factors affecting the training program.

Consider this: a course designer and developer was assigned to prepare product training for new software. When assigned to this project, the SMEs said that two-thirds of the users of this product worked in hospitals and the other third worked in universities. After checking actual sales, this course designer and developer learned that few people who actually used the software worked in hospitals. Universities made up about 60 percent of the market and manufacturers accounted for most of the remaining 40 percent. Had the course designer and developer not verified the information, the product training would have been geared toward the wrong audience.

To avoid a similar situation in which you target the wrong audience or similarly go off-track, start a training project by first verifying the information that you received and then filling in missing, but useful, information. Specifically, you need to learn about the following categories of issues:

- the request itself
- the business need underlying the project
- the desired performance
- the current performance
- the tasks in desired and current performance
- the learners and the influences on them
- issues affecting learning and its application in the work environment
- product and project constraints affecting the program.

Collecting and verifying information about a project and determining how to translate that information into goals for the training project are the main activities of a needs analysis. This chapter targets the information you need to conduct this analysis.

After collecting the information, you assess it and use that assessment to establish goals for the project. Trainers state goals for a project as objectives and, immediately after writing objectives, develop tests (assessments) to assess whether learners have achieved them. Writing objectives and tests complete the analysis process; the next chapter explores these two tasks.

Issue 1. Restate and Clarify the Request

The first issue in analyzing the needs underlying a request to develop a training program is restating and clarifying the request for it.

Starting the project using the exact same words that the sponsor used lets the sponsor know that you listened carefully to the request—and heard it. Few things build trust the way that type of listening does. For example, if a sponsor asked you to "develop a two-part sales training course, one of which focuses on the product and another that focuses on techniques for relationship marketing," begin this part by stating that you have been asked to develop a "two-part sales training course,

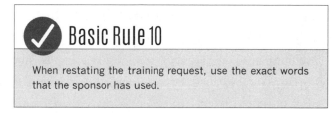

Basic Rule 10

When restating the training request, use the exact words that the sponsor has used.

one of which focuses on the product and another that focuses on techniques for relationship marketing." You might expand on the request after quoting the sponsor's predefined specifications verbatim.

Repeating the request using the sponsor's words does not mean that the final project must take the form of the request. For example, if a sponsor requests that you design and develop a one-week classroom course, but you believe that the sponsor's needs would be best served by creating a preclass workbook and a two-day classroom course, the sponsor is more likely to follow your suggestions if he believes that you understood the initial request.

Only restate the request if you believe you understand it. If something about the request confuses you, clarify it with the sponsor before restating the request. In fact, clear up any questions about the specific request and the intended learners before moving forward with the project. Although inquiring about other areas in the needs analysis also explores these issues, clarifying your basic understanding of the request now makes sure that you're asking the right questions later.

When restating the request, also include key parts of the request that affect course design. Here are three examples of restated requests:

- The vice president of marketing and sales has requested a one-week classroom-based sales school, a series of workbooks to address prerequisite skills, and some postclass content to help learners apply the material on the job. The sales school must cover relationship marketing, marketing policies, and ordering procedures and provide an overview of the current product line.
- The manager of internal software applications has requested a half-day training course for end users of the new accounts receivable application. The course must launch on May 2, three weeks before the new application goes live.
- The chief security officer has requested a two-hour classroom-based training course for managers about the new security policy. The course must launch in eight weeks, when new security procedures begin.

Issue 2. Identify the Business Need Underlying the Request

In their 2008 book, *Training for Impact,* Dana and James Robinson advise training and talent development professionals that sponsors are most likely to value their efforts—and that these efforts are most likely to lead to change—if trainers directly tie their programs to a business need. A business need refers to a goal or activity fundamental to the success of the organization, such as meeting a sales goal, reducing the cost of serving clients, and maintaining ongoing operations.

Three categories of business needs exist: generating revenue, containing expenses (that is, helping to reduce the costs of rework or inefficient processes), or complying with regulations (that is, adhering to a rule or guideline from a government, industry, association, or organization). And the best time to identify this business need is at the very beginning of the effort to develop a training program, before you even consider which skills it should develop.

Basic Rule 11

Before determining what content to include, start each training project by identifying the business need.

Only choose one—and only one—business need. Programs with two business needs have two focus points, thus increasing the risk that the program will not achieve either. Consider, for example, a user training course intended to both generate revenue (by showing how easily people use a product) and contain expenses (by making users more self-sufficient). To avoid worrying prospective customers, the course might not include a troubleshooting unit. But by dropping that unit the course loses one of the key means of building the self-sufficiency of users, and users thus do not learn how to solve common problems on their own.

Basic Rule 12

Choose one—and only one—business need for a single project. The different business needs compete with one another, and having two or more obscures the focus of the project—and reduces its effectiveness.

After identifying the business need, state it as tangibly as possible without overpromising results. Here are possible business needs (goals) for three examples described previously in this chapter:

- *Generating revenue:* After completing the proposed sales school, 90 percent of new marketing representatives will meet their first-year revenue goals.
- *Containing expenses:* After completing the training course for the new accounts receivable application, 85 percent of workers in the accounts receivable organization will transfer to the new application by June 1, thus reducing application support costs by 10 percent.
- *Complying with regulations:* After completing the training course on the new security policy, the organization will have 100 percent compliance with the new security procedures within four weeks of their launch.

When stating business needs, avoid making promises that cannot be met. For example, if you have been asked to develop a training program that supports a sales effort, the business need might be meeting the sales projections. Don't promise that the program will increase sales higher than the projections by the marketing group.

If you struggle to identify a connection between the program and a business need of the organization, the sponsor might not really need the program.

 Think About This

Avoid confusing the business need with the business case. The business case is an economic justification for producing the course. The business need is just one part of that case.

Issue 3. Describe the Desired Performance

To start building the desired performance, you need three pieces of information: a narrative description of desired performance, a narrative description of current performance (to contrast with desired performance), and detailed listings of tasks in current and desired performance.

Desired performance refers to the way that sponsors would like for learners to complete their job-related tasks after the training program. By starting at the end—desired performance—you can keep that goal in mind while designing and developing the program, and you can avoid covering irrelevant material.

Sponsors often describe desired performance in terms of measures that learners achieve when they perform optimally, called *performance indicators.* Consider these performance indicators for the three examples:

- *New sales school:* Using their knowledge of the entire product line, sales representatives will use relationship marketing techniques to sell all relevant products to their assigned customers and generate follow-up sales from at least 50 percent of those customers within one year.
- *New accounts receivable application:* Users will transfer their accounting information to the new system by June 1 and will use the system without assistance by June 15, requiring no more than 0.5 calls for assistance a month.
- *New security policy:* Confidential material will not be leaked. More specifically, all written confidential material will be properly labeled (both online and in print). All confidential material will be locked in desks or credenzas, even in secured areas. No confidential material will be discussed in public areas. To gain access to all confidential material on internal computers, users will have to enter a password.

But successfully achieving desired performance involves more than simply achieving a metric. It also involves learning to comfortably operate within a particular environment. So when describing desired performance, you need to describe more

Basic Rule 13

Before you determine what to teach, you first need to determine what desired performance looks like.

than the performance indicators. You need to also describe the environment in which people achieve desired performance and some of the motivations underlying it. Presenting the description of the desired behavior as a scenario—a snapshot of performance—helps you gain some insight into why the learners might perform in a particular manner as well as which factors could support performance and which ones, if not carefully addressed, could limit the ability of learners to achieve the desired performance. Consider the example in Figure 3-1, which describes a scenario of desired performance for the sales school requested by the vice president of marketing.

Scenarios provide a clear description of the desired performance as well as insights into the conditions under which learners must perform when they apply the skills in the real world. You might need to address these conditions in the training program. Or, because of the conditions identified, you might need to develop supporting materials that help learners apply the skills on the job.

Issue 4. Describe Current Performance

After describing desired performance, write a corresponding scenario that describes the current performance of learners. This is the second of three pieces of information that help you determine which material to address in the training program. Consider the example in Figure 3-2 of current performance for the sales school requested by the vice president of marketing.

Note that most training programs build on current performance. But you might be assigned to a training program for which no current performance exists. For example, you might develop training for a new organization that has no track record, or for a completely new product or service that the organization has never offered. In such rare instances, you would skip the scenario of current performance.

Figure 3-1. Scenario of Desired Performance

[Start with the performance indicator.] James, a first-year sales representative, meets his sales quota.

[Describe in detail a scenario of performance. Make sure to fictionalize the details.] James has recently joined Mega Corporation as a sales representative, where he is responsible for selling office supplies to large and medium-size organizations in greater Cincinnati. Most customers purchase office supplies centrally and prefer to handle purchasing online through the company's website, without working through a sales representative. So to strengthen customer relationships with the company, Mega Corporation has its sales representatives go through a one-week sales training program with some postclass review to cover relationship marketing, marketing policies, and ordering procedures.

With the knowledge from the training program in mind, James recognizes that sales calls to existing customers are not redundant. He thus calls on his customers at least once per quarter, and he ends up spending 80 percent of his time on maintaining existing customer relationships. Each Monday morning, he downloads the sales history for the customer he intends to call and checks the business news service to find out about the business situation of the customer, which might affect purchasing ability. He prepares a list of products that might meet the customer's needs but that do not appear on the order list.

During customer meetings, James starts by thanking customers for their business. He asks them about their current needs and responds by suggesting additional products that might be useful to them, often mentioned information he read on the news service. Each week James also thanks the customers with whom he met the previous week for their time, further strengthening their relationship.

Because he received a safe sales territory, James was likely to meet his sales quota anyway. But because he followed the techniques taught in the training program—preparing for the customer meeting, thanking customers for their business, listening to their needs, and suggesting products based on his knowledge of their operations—James is able to exceed his sales quota by 5 percent.

Figure 3-2. Scenario of Current Performance

[Start with the performance indicator. Note the difference in meeting quota from ideal performance.] James, a first-year sales representative, falls short of his sales quota by 15 percent.

[Describe in detail a scenario of performance. Make sure to fictionalize the details.] James has recently joined Mega Corporation as a sales representative, where he is responsible for selling office supplies to large and medium-size organizations in greater Cincinnati. Most customers purchase office supplies centrally and prefer to handle purchasing online through the company's website, without working through a sales representative.

[Note the difference in sales approach—from a focus on keeping current customers to one on prospecting new customers.] Because existing customers can handle their own reordering online and he has easy access to their sales records from the company sales system, James does not regularly call on them. He feels that such calls are redundant and is not sure what he would tell them anyway. Instead, he identifies organizations in his territory that do not use Mega Corporation as their preferred office supplier and cold-calls them. He typically shows up unannounced and requests a meeting with the purchasing agent. Three-quarters of the time, these purchasing agents refuse to meet with James and will not schedule a meeting.

[Note the different results.] Because he received a safe territory for his starting position, James should have easily met his sales quota. But as a result of his ineffective sales methods, he falls 15 percent short of his sales quota.

But assuming you prepare scenarios of current and desired performance, you would compare them to determine the performance gap. The training program should address this gap: the difference between the two. See Figure 3-3 for an example description of a performance gap for the sales school.

Figure 3-3. Description of a Performance Gap

Many first-year sales representatives at Mega Corporation miss their sales targets. Instead of focusing on maintaining and expanding sales with existing customers, they prospect for new ones, often through ineffective cold-calls. They believe that because current customers use the online order system, interactions with them are not necessary.

The new sales representatives are also unprepared for sales calls and, as a result, cannot make targeted suggestions that meet their needs. In some cases, the sales representatives inadvertently insult the customers with the off-the-mark suggestions. They're unprepared because they fail to check the sales history of and recent news about the customer's organization. They do not inquire about customer needs, much less listen to them. Most important, they do not have a structured—but flexible—framework for presenting products to prospective customers that allows them to give a professional presentation but, at the same time, easily tailor the framework to different organizations. In addition, most do not schedule formal appointments in advance; they just show up unannounced at the customer's door.

Issue 5. Conduct a Task Analysis

After identifying the performance gap, identify the sequence of tasks that learners should follow to achieve the desired performance and how that compares with the sequence of tasks currently followed. Identifying the specific tasks involved in desired and current performance is called a task analysis.

 Basic Rule 14

Identify each task that someone must go through to achieve desired performance, so that you can address those tasks in the training program.

For many course designers and developers, this is the most complex job in a needs analysis because it involves several subresponsibilities. You start by identifying general tasks in desired performance, categorizing tasks in desired performance, writing tasks as precisely as possible, and sequencing tasks by placing them in a hierarchy. You then continue by creating a similar list of tasks in current performance and comparing that with desired performance. You conclude by identifying entry skills that all the intended learners are assumed to have already mastered.

Issue 5-A. Identify General Tasks in Desired Performance

The first thing to do when conducting a task analysis is identify the general tasks that workers must do to achieve the desired performance. In the best circumstances, the sponsor or one of the SMEs can name these tasks. But in most cases, they can only name a few. That's because the sponsor and SMEs do not perform the tasks as workers do. For new products, policies, and procedures, sponsors and SMEs can only describe the performance conceptually; they often overlook practical issues that arise when performing the tasks in everyday conditions. So you need to determine desired performance on your own.

Three key sources provide a starting point for doing so. The first source is the description of performance gap that resulted from preparing the scenarios of desired and current performance. This description identifies processes that workers either omit or perform poorly.

The second source is the documentation published by the organization that describes the procedures that workers should follow when performing the task. Typically, for training intended to improve existing products, policies, and procedures, such documentation exists and is known by names like Standard Operating Procedures, Policies and Procedures, and Documentation. For new products, policies, and procedures, plans or notes might be available. Even when documentation is available, the descriptions, policies, and procedures are often at odds with performance desired by the sponsor and the documentation must be corrected while developing the training.

 Think About This

Tasks fall into three categories:

- *Psychomotor* tasks are those performed by hand or involving some other physical activity.
- *Cognitive* tasks are performed mentally, such as choosing the right model of computer to meet a customer's needs or matching symptoms with a diagnosis.
- *Affective* tasks are associated with learners' attitudes. They are usually redefined as cognitive or psychomotor tasks that reflect the behavior of someone who assumes the attitude, such as adopting a smoke-free life by choosing not to try cigarettes.

This categorization provides early insights into the nature of the instructional material a training program should cover.

The third source is expert performers, people who already perform in the desired way. They can explain how they perform tasks, variations in desired performance under different conditions of work, and roadblocks that others face on the road to desired performance.

As you identify the tasks, formally prepare a list. The tasks should appear in the order in which workers should perform them.

Issue 5-B. Categorize Tasks in Desired Performance

When preparing the list of tasks that workers must master, consider these task categories:

- Desired end result, which is the major task that learners need to learn how to perform and the performance indicated described earlier hints at it.
- Foundational concepts, which provide learners with a framework for approaching the task.
- Basic processes for performing tasks.
- Alternate processes, which are others ways of performing basic processes. Although you should maintain an awareness of these alternate processes, introducing more than one to learners when first teaching them how to perform the basic processes will only confuse them.
- Common issues, which learners need to know how to handle to increase their self-sufficiency on the job.

Figure 3-4 presents an example of these categories from the sales school.

Figure 3-4. An Initial List of Tasks

Task Category	Sales School Example
Desired end result	Sell Mega Corporation products to the intended customers.
Foundational concepts	Relationship marketing, which assumes that the best customer and the one requiring the least effort is an existing customer, focuses on building and maintaining relationships with customers, and uses the acts of listening to customer needs and meeting those needs as the basis for a solid customer relationship.
Basic processes	• Set up appointments with existing customers in advance and confirm those appointments. • Prepare for the calls by reviewing the sales record and news, and preparing suggestions of possible interest to the customer. • Meet with customers to discuss their needs. • Follow up with a thank you note. • Prospect for new clients on a limited basis, but handle similarly.

(continued)

Figure 3-4. An Initial List of Tasks (continued)

Task Category	Sales School Example
Alternate processes	This is an introductory course; to avoid confusing learners, no alternate processes will be mentioned.
Common issues	Explain how to handle common issues that arise when performing the task, which increases the self-sufficiency of learners when they attempt to apply the skills on the job. In the case of the sales school, learners might learn how to respond to common concerns raised by customers, such as "This product doesn't meet my needs" and "That sounds interesting but we have a tight budget this year."

Issue 5-C. Write Tasks as Precisely as Possible

After jotting down the tasks, refine them to be as precise as possible. Revise the tasks so each one begins with an action verb. An action verb describes a task in a way that a third party can observe whether the person completed it, and all parties would agree on the assessment. For example, "schedule" is an action verb.

When refining the tasks, limit each task to one—and only one—action. For example, setting up and confirming appointments with customers represents two separate tasks: (1) setting up appointments with customers and (2) confirming appointments with customers. Do not combine them.

Note, too, that refining the tasks is an ongoing process. You continue doing so while designing and developing the training program because you become increasingly familiar with the instructional material and can make it increasingly more precise.

Issue 5-D. Create a Sequence and Hierarchy for Tasks

As you evaluate the tasks, you might notice that some need to occur before others (a sequence). You might also notice that some tasks are actually pieces of a larger, more complex task. For example, to set up an appointment with a customer, one needs to first determine which customers have not been visited this quarter, find contact information for them, and determine some preferred dates for meeting with them. This suggests that tasks follow both a sequence and a hierarchy.

At the top of the hierarchy are the most important tasks, called *main tasks*. A training program typically covers between five and nine main tasks. It may have fewer, but if it has more than nine main tasks, the amount of material may become overwhelming to learners. If you find that you have more than nine main tasks, consider combining these tasks.

Think About This

Avoid abstract verbs when writing tasks. Abstract verbs are ones that cannot be observed by an outside party. These include two terms closely associated with learning: *know* and *understand*. Third parties cannot observe knowing and understanding; they can only observe products of knowing and understanding, such as recall of facts, explanations of concepts, and analyses of reports. So never use *know* and *understand* when writing tasks. Replace them with action verbs. For example, what can learners do when they understand something? Can they explain? Describe? Define? All are more precise than *know* and *understand*. Later, the more precise terms will help you better focus the training program.

To perform one main task, learners must often master several related tasks, called *supporting tasks*. Typically, each main task has between three and nine supporting tasks. Some supporting tasks, in turn, have their own supporting tasks, called sub-supporting tasks.

Sometimes, learners would need more specific information about the tasks than main and supporting tasks can convey. In such instances, you can extend the hierarchy further down, into sub-supporting tasks, sub-sub supporting tasks, and so on. Some task hierarchies can go into seven or eight levels of depth. Figure 3-5 shows the sequence and hierarchy for the desired performance for the sales school.

Figure 3-5. Sequence and Hierarchy of Tasks

End Result: Sell Mega Corporation products to the prospective customers.	
Main Tasks	**Supporting and Sub-Supporting Tasks**

Explain the benefits of using relationship marketing as the framework for the sales process (the foundational framework).	1. Describe relationship marketing.
	  a. Define the term relationship marketing.
	  b. Explain the key components of *relationship marketing*.
	2. Contrast relationship marketing with other types of marketing.
	  a. Define cold-calling-based sales.
	  b. Define an inbound-based approach to sales.
	3. State the benefits of relationship marketing over other types of marketing.
	  a. Explain that relationship marketing emphasizes matching customers with products and services that meet their needs.
	  b. Explain that relationship marketing emphasizes existing customers and ongoing relationships.
	  c. Explain that relationship marketing offers a more efficient use of time than other types of marketing.

(continued)

Figure 3-5. Sequence and Hierarchy of Tasks (continued)

End Result: Sell Mega Corporation products to the prospective customers.	
Main Tasks	**Supporting and Sub-Supporting Tasks**

Follow a relationship-based process to sell to customers (the basic process).	1. Maintain ongoing relationships with existing customers.
	  a. Each quarter, schedule meetings with current customers.
	  b. Prepare for the meeting.
	  c. Retrieve the most recent sales report for the customer from the Customer Information System.
	  d. On the sales report, identify purchasing trends.
	  e. Meet with customers to discuss their needs.
	  f. Within two business days of the meeting, send a thank you note to the customer.
	2. Establish relationships with new customers.

Handle common problems that might arise in a sales call (the common issues).	1. Describe a process for handling objections.
	  a. When hearing an objection, restate it to verify that you have correctly heard it.
	  b. After confirming that you heard the objection correctly, state features, advantages, and benefits of your products and services that address the concerns.
	  c. Verify with the customer that you have addressed the concern.
	  d. If the customer says that you have addressed the concern, end this part of the discussion.
	  e. If the customer says that you have not addressed the concern, repeat this process until you have.

Issue 5-E. Create a Similar List of Tasks for Current Performance

After creating the list of tasks in desired performance, create a similar list of tasks that reflect how the intended learners currently perform. Use the same process followed to create the list of tasks in desired performance: identify general tasks in current performance, categorize tasks in current performance (such as a foundational concept or a basic process), write tasks as precisely as possible, and sequence tasks in current performance and place them in a hierarchy.

One of the challenges of creating the list of tasks in current performance is describing it in terms of tasks that others can observe. Many course designers and developers tend to describe performance in terms of what the intended learners do not do. Doing so does not describe performance; it describes what is not happening.

For example, a course designer and developer might be tempted to express the first main task as follows: "Does not follow a relationship marketing as the framework for the sales process." But that is not correct. A more accurate example would be: "Relies on cold-calling and inbound-based approaches to sales."

Issue 5-F. Compare Current and Desired Performance

Review the list of tasks in current and desired performance to determine where they are identical, similar, slightly different, and completely different. When developing the training program later, you will need to move learners from the way that they currently perform to the desired performance and these observations will help you develop a strategy for doing so.

Issue 5-G. Identify Entry Tasks

After comparing current and desired performance and determining which tasks learners need to perform differently, determine which tasks learners should have already mastered before starting the program and thus will not be addressed by the training program. Tasks already mastered and not covered by the training program are called *entry tasks*. Entry tasks become the basis for prerequisite skills learners should have mastered before starting the training program.

Issue 6. Describe the Learners and the Influences on Them

Information about the learners is as important as information about the tasks. Prepare two types of information about learners: general background information about the learners and brief narrative descriptions of three distinct learners.

 Basic Rule 15

Collect enough information about learners to "know" them. The better you understand who your learners are, their previous experience, and their motivations, the better you can tailor the instructional material to their needs.

Issue 6-A. General Background Information

General background information provides some broad insights into those who will participate in the training program. When collecting general information, course designers and developers typically seek:

- Demographic data, including job title, length of experience, assumed knowledge, sex (if relevant), age range (if appropriate), language skills (if relevant), cultural affiliations (if appropriate), and similar information.
- Previous knowledge and experience about the topic of the proposed training program or with related material, which helps you avoid repeating material learners already know and anticipate concerns that could affect their learning the new material.

- Influences affecting learners, including organizational influences, such as a recent reorganization that results in new work for a group, and cultural influences, such as different geographic regions or countries in which the organization plans to offer the training.

Issue 6-B. Narrative Descriptions of Three Learners

Although general background information provides broad insights into the intended learners, this information lacks the specific insights that will be helpful in meaningfully connecting with learners. Narrative descriptions—much like the descriptions of desired and current performance—can provide additional insight.

The idea of creating narrative descriptions of intended learners (technically called *personas*) comes from the field of user experience design. Alan Cooper, Robert Reimann, David Cronin, and Christopher Noessel (2014) suggest that these narratives provide designers with vivid mental images of their learners when designing programs and those mental images help designers address emotional needs that demographics and general information often overlook. They suggest writing narrative descriptions of three learners: a high-maintenance learner who requires exceptional attention from the instructor; a low-maintenance learner who requires little attention; and a third, middle-of-the-road learner, who requires an average amount of attention. By describing these three, they suggest that designers will have encompassed the needs of most learners. Figure 3-6 provides a narrative of one learner for the sales school, one who requires exceptional attention from instructors.

Figure 3-6. Example of a Narrative Description of a Low-Maintenance Learner

Fresh from completing a bachelor's degree in business administration from State U, James joined Mega Corporation as a sales representative in the business products division, where he is responsible for selling office supplies to large and medium-size organizations in greater Cincinnati. A slightly above-average student at State U, James prided himself on his ability to coast through classes, often waiting until the last minute to study and pulling all-nighters. He would spend most of his time organizing meet-and-greets with recent alums and shopping for business attire so he would look "professional" at meetings. James was very excited to receive the offer from Mega Corporation, but he now focuses more on his new business wardrobe than on his work; it takes his mind off of the anxiety he feels about the sales quota has to meet. Although he would seem like a candidate who would pay close attention in class, James thinks he is already in the field and often tunes out the lecture to check on messages from the two customers already assigned to him.

Issue 7. Identify Issues Affecting Learning and Its Application in the Work Environment

In addition to specific information about the performance, tasks, and learners, also identify issues in the organization that could affect learning and its application to the work environment.

Some issues affect the learning process itself. Most of these are environmental factors. If the sponsor expects a classroom course, for instance, some characteristics of the classroom could affect the learning process, such as noise, poor air circulation, and inconvenient locations. If the sponsor requested a self-study course, determine whether the organization plans to set aside work time for learners to study and provide quiet spaces to do so. If the sponsor wants learners to practice skills on real equipment as part of the training, determine whether the equipment is likely to be moved into the classroom or is physically nearby, or if a field trip to another location is needed.

Some issues affect the ability of learners to apply learning on the job. Many sponsors might lead you to believe that the organization is excited about the changes training might bring. But verify that claim as workers often feel differently. Inquire about the general attitude of learners and others in the organization toward the instructional material, and anticipate whether they will embrace the changes and why.

Also consider how the supervisors might respond to the changes. Research shows that supportive supervisors play a critical role in whether learners ultimately apply material learned in training on the job. Consider, too, the organization's history with change by asking about previous change efforts. Assess how the changes to be brought by this training program might reflect past successful and unsuccessful efforts.

Issue 8. Identify Product and Project Constraints Affecting the Program

Constraints are requirements that affect the way you develop the training program. They affect how it must be developed (product constraints) and the time and funding available to develop the program (project constraints).

Basic Rule 16

Identify the constraints affecting the program—product related (ones affecting the design and development of the program) and project related (ones affecting the time and funds available to develop the program).

Product Constraints

Product constraints affect the manner in which you present the program, its appearance, and the tools (software) you use to create it. Typical product constraints include editorial guidelines, design guidelines, technical guidelines, and templates.

Editorial guidelines: When writing the text of the training program, most organizations have guidelines on the use of terminology, punctuation, and grammar. For example, some organizations prefer that course designers and developers spell out the word *percent* while others prefer the percentage sign %. In most instances, training programs must conform to these editorial guidelines.

Editorial guidelines are generally compiled in *style guides,* and most organizations have a preferred guide that staff consult to determine how to handle editorial issues. Most organizations use a third-party style guide, such as *The Chicago Manual of Style* or *APA Style.* But because these style guides only handle general issues, organizations may develop extensions—additional guidelines—that address organization-specific issues, such as the proper way of handling the names of products and services provided by the organization. Most organizations also have a preferred dictionary, which resolves questions about spelling and usage.

Design guidelines: Many organizations establish a standard structure for particular types of courses. For example, some organizations always begin live training programs with a title slide that has a particular look, an agenda slide, a slide that provides administrative details, and a closing slide. Other organizations prefer particular instructional techniques to present particular types of instructional material. Still other organizations conclude all self-study programs with a summary, a test, descriptions of related courses, a glossary, an index, and an evaluation form.

Most organizations want a "family look" to everything they publish, so that materials produced by many different groups within the organization and for many different purposes appear to have the same publisher. This unified look is one element of the organization's brand and is the centerpiece of design guidelines. These guidelines also indicate when and how to use the organization logo (where in the program it should appear, where to place it on the screen, slide, or page, and how it should appear).

Technical guidelines: In addition to editorial and design guidelines, most organizations establish technical guidelines to identify the software that's used to design, develop, and deliver training programs. Typical software specified in technical guidelines usually include the preferred word processor (such as Microsoft Word); presentation graphics program (such as Microsoft PowerPoint); graphics, illustration, and photo retouching programs for preparing images (such as Adobe Illustrator and Photoshop); slidecasting software for creating online and mobile self-study programs (such as Articulate Storyline or Camtasia Studio); and audio and video editing software to refine recordings.

Organizations also identify the software they prefer to use to deliver courses to learners. Organizations deliver most self-study courses to learners through a web browser, like Google Chrome and Mozilla Firefox. For courses conducted live and online—in which learners meet instructors at a particular web location at a designated time and where instructors can show slides and other documents, and speak and interact with learners—organizations identify the software used for that virtual classroom, such as Adobe Connect and WebEx.

Templates: To simplify compliance with editorial and design guidelines, many organizations create templates. A template is like a fill-in-the-blank form that either covers particular screens, entire units, or entire courses. Templates prompt course designers and developers for particular types of information in particular places and might even state how to enter the information. The system then formats the information so that it follows the intended guidelines and that screens, slides, and pages appear a particular way, minimizing the design effort on the part of course designers and developers.

Project Constraints

Project constraints affect the resources available to create the project, including the drop-dead deadline for completing the project, the not-to-exceed budget, and the staff who must participate in the design and development effort. They become the basis for developing a schedule and budget for the training program.

In addition to gathering these project constraints, also gather one additional set of project constraints—one you should *not* include in a report to sponsors: the previous history of projects with this sponsor. Does the organization meet its schedules? Is the organization notorious for last-minute changes? If the best predictor of future behavior is past behavior, being aware of a tendency for lateness and last-minute changes can help you devise strategies for dealing with such issues before they arise (such as adding fudge factors to schedules, as suggested in chapter 2).

Four Methods of Uncovering Needs

When conducting a needs analysis, you ultimately want to *triangulate* information. That is, rather than relying on one source for all your information (at the best, that source might not be complete; at the worst, it might not be trustworthy), you want to collect information from a variety of sources, at least three (hence, the *tri* in triangulation). By looking at the content from several vantages, you can construct a more realistic portrait of the needs. The following sections describe four ways you might be able to quickly and easily get the information you need at this point in a project.

Talk

Conduct formal interviews with as many people as possible, including stakeholders such as the sponsor, SMEs, and prospective learners. Other stakeholders probably have an interest in the proposed training program, too, and will happily share their thoughts. The advantage of interviews is that you can collect information from many stakeholders and receive an extensive amount of information in a limited period of time. The disadvantage is that the information received is biased, representing the viewpoint of the interviewee, one person might contradict another, and information might not be accurate.

Focus

Focus groups are a special type of interview, in which you interview eight to 12 demographically similar people at a single time. The focus group usually lasts two hours, and it might cover three to seven questions (with so many people, you're not likely to have time for more questions).

An outside facilitator usually leads the focus group and makes sure that each participant has an opportunity to speak. The advantage of a focus group is its efficiency; you can interview many people in less than the time it would take to interview them individually. The disadvantage is that the participants are not able to exchange much information, and group pressure might prevent some from speaking candidly.

Experience

One of the ways to learn about a subject is to experience it. You can follow people through their daily routines from the start of a workday until its end. Course designers and developers typically follow an expert, a novice, or both, in the performance of the tasks covered by the proposed program. The advantage of this approach is the hands-on nature of the experience and the depth to which a course designer and developer can see the tasks in action. The disadvantages are the cost (especially if travel is required) and that the day only reflects one person's experience—and just one day of it.

Note that if you only have part of a day, a little observation is better than none. In other words, if you don't have time to follow around an expert or novice for a whole day, perhaps you might be able to do so for a few hours.

Read

In many cases, you do not need to conduct new research to uncover the information needed to start a training project—you merely need to familiarize yourself with existing materials. Therefore, one of the most valuable sources for a needs analysis is the documents already available about the situation. Read anything that might provide useful insights into the tasks, learners, environment, and constraints: reports, plans, policies, user's guides, memos and other correspondence, trade magazines, and even other training programs. The advantage of this method is that it unearths much good information. The disadvantage is that most people recognize that written records are permanent and prepare them so that they reflect most positively on the situation.

Platinum, Silver, and Bronze Types of Projects

The analysis process described in this chapter reflects a platinum approach. When conducting an analysis for a silver or bronze project, you often rely on fewer sources of information about the situation than suggested here. The descriptions of desired and current performance and the tasks might be condensed. A silver project might only include a description of desired performance and a condensed list of tasks, and a bronze project only a description of tasks. Silver and bronze projects might only include demographics about learners rather than scenarios. Both silver and bronze projects would include descriptions of the learning environment and constraints, as these issues arise in all three types of projects.

Some silver and bronze projects involve revising existing training programs. Although course designers and developers verify that earlier analyses conducted for the projects are still relevant, the primary focus of the analysis for a revision is on new tasks to include in the revised program and any new groups of learners who might now use the program.

Getting It Done

Although the chapter describes the eight issues to consider when conducting a needs analysis, remember that no single set of scripted questions can identify all the needs underlying a project. So if you hear of something that you feel might be relevant, explore it.

As you conduct a needs analysis, keep an open mind as you explore needs. If you enter an analysis with the solution already designed, you will not ask the questions that might help you develop the training program best matched to meet the needs. Keep an open mind, too, about the answers to the questions. Rather than entering this process to confirm your answers, use it to learn. You might find that your instincts are off track and because you have not yet developed the program, you can easily change strategies at this point.

Use Exercise 3-1 to guide the results of the needs analysis of a project on which you are currently working.

Exercise 3-1. The Eight Issues to Consider When Conducting a Needs Analysis

Needs Analysis Issue	Actions Required	Information Source(s)
1. Restate the request	Use the sponsor's exact words. _____ _____ _____ _____ _____	Sponsor
2. Identify the business need	This project will provide the following benefit to the sponsor (check one box only): ❑ Generate revenue ❑ Contain expenses ❑ Comply with regulations How will this training program provide this benefit to the sponsor? (Explain as tangibly as possible.) _____ _____ _____ _____ _____	Interviews (list individuals) _____ _____ Documents (list them) _____ _____ Other (list) _____
3. Describe desired performance as a scenario	Start with the performance indicator: . _____ Describe in detail a scenario of performancer: _____ _____ _____ _____ _____	Interviews (list individuals) _____ _____ Documents (list them) _____ _____ Other (list) _____ _____

(continued)

Exercise 3-1. The Eight Issues to Consider When Conducting a Needs Analysis (continued)

Needs Analysis Issue	Actions Required	Information Source(s)
4. Describe current performance	Start with the performance indicator: _____ Describe in detail a scenario of performance: _____ Describe the performance gap: End result:_____ Foundational concepts:_____ Basic processes:_____ Alternate processes:_____ Common issues: _____ _____	Interviews (list individuals) _____ Documents (list them) _____ Other (list) _____ _____ _____ _____
5. Conduct a task analysis	**Desired performance** / **Current performance** End result: _____ / End result:_____ Main task 1: _____ / Main task 1: _____ Supporting tasks: / Supporting tasks: Main task 2: _____ / Main task 2:_____ Supporting tasks: / Supporting tasks:	Interviews (list individuals) _____ Documents (list them) _____ Other (list) _____

Exercise 3-1. The Eight Issues to Consider When Conducting a Needs Analysis (continued)

Needs Analysis Issue	Actions Required	Information Source(s)
6. Describe the learners and the influences on them	1. Background information: • Demographics: _____ • Previous knowledge: _____ • Influences: _____ 2. Descriptions of three learners (write as narratives) • Learner who requires extra attention from the instructor _____ _____ • Learner who requires average amount of attention from the instructor _____ • Learner who requires surprisingly little attention from the instructor _____ _____	Interviews (list individuals) _____ Documents (list them) _____ _____ _____ Other (list) _____ _____
7. Identify issues affecting learning and its application in the work environment	• Issues affecting learning _____ _____ • Issues affecting the application of learning in the work environment _____ _____ _____	Interviews (list individuals) Documents (list them) _____ Other (list) _____

8. Identify product and project constraints affecting the program	1. Product constraints:
	• Editorial guidelines:
	  Style guide:_____
	  Dictionary: _____
	• Design guidelines: _____
	• Technical guidelines:_____
	• Templates: _____
	2. Project constraints:
	• Must-meet deadline:_____
	• Not-to-exceed budget: _____
	• Must-include staff:_____
	• Corporate culture and project history (do not share with sponsor):
	
	_____
		Interviews (list individuals)
		
		_____
		
		_____
		
		_____
		
		Documents (list them)
		
		_____
		
		_____
		Other (list)
		
		_____

4

The Basic Instructional Objective

 What's Inside This Chapter

This chapter covers the latter stages in the analysis phase: translating the needs identified into instructional objectives with observable and measurable goals for the training program, and writing evaluation materials like tests to assess the extent to which the program achieved its goals. (Yes, you write the tests before developing course materials.) Specifically, this chapter addresses:

- The basic value of objectives and evaluations
- The basics of establishing objectives, such as determining which skills learners must master, writing objectives, and distinguishing among main and supporting objectives
- The basics of drafting evaluations for a training program using the Kirkpatrick model, which involves assessing reaction, learning, and transfer to the job
- The basics of presenting the analysis and requirements to sponsors for their review and approval.

An exercise at the end of this chapter guides you through the process of preparing objectives and evaluations for a project on which you are working.

The Basic Value of Objectives and Evaluation

In the needs analysis, you verified a request for training and learned about the business needs underlying it, the desired performance, the skills learners must master, who the learners are, issues that could affect learning, and the product and project constraints. So you're ready to begin designing the training program. Right?

Not quite.

Although you have identified the needs and determined what the training program should accomplish, you need to formally state the goals for the program. By establishing these goals, both you and your sponsor have a common agreement about the purpose of the program and the skills it should develop.

Immediately after setting the goals—and before any work begins on the training program—draft the instruments used to assess whether the program achieved these objectives: satisfaction surveys, tests, and follow-up surveys. As learning expert Robert Mager (1997) advised, do this now because if the objectives state what the training program should do, then the evaluation instruments should describe what successful achievement of those objectives looks like.

 **Basic Rule 17**

Before beginning any formal work on a training program, formally state the objectives for it, and then prepare the evaluations, such as tests, which assess whether the objectives have been achieved.

This chapter explains how to perform these activities. The first part explains how to write objectives—the formal statements of goals. The second part explains how to draft evaluations. And the third part explains how to present the analysis and requirements to your sponsor for approval.

Establishing Objectives

Objectives state the goals that a proposed training program must achieve. More specifically, objectives state the skills that the training program must develop and the extent to which learners must master those skills. Writing objectives is a widely followed practice among trainers. According to some studies, nearly 100 percent of all trainers prepare objectives as part of designing a program.

Determining the Skills That Learners Must Master

Two categories of information gathered in the needs analysis help you determine the skills that a training program must address. The first is the overall desired performance, which then becomes the overall goal for the program. The second is the specific skills leaners must master to achieve the overall desired performance.

The overall desired performance for a training program is the end result: what learners must accomplish. Because much of the design process focuses on specific skills and related details, trainers often lose sight of the end result. Formally stating the end result provides a point of reference and helps designers retain a clear focus. Figure 4-1 demonstrates how to translate the desired performance, as stated in chapter 3, into an end result.

Figure 4-1. Translating Desired Performance Into End Results

Example 1: New Sales School

Here is the desired performance for the new sales school:

> *Using relationship marketing techniques, new sales representatives (those with one year or less of experience) will sell all relevant products to their assigned customers.*

Note how the term *new sales representative* is defined in a way that it can be externally verified. Also note that, although the original purpose of the program included properly completing forms, this was dropped to ensure that the original purpose has a clearer singular focus. Furthermore, if sales representatives incorrectly process orders, they are not likely to have repeat customers. And note that the phrase "using their knowledge of the product line" does not appear in the statement of desired performance. Sales representatives cannot sell relevant products unless they can match products from the entire product line with specific customer needs.

Example 2: New Accounts Receivable Application

Here is the desired performance of the new accounts receivable application:

> *Users will process all accounts receivables without assistance using the new system by June 15, requiring no more than 0.5 calls for assistance a month).*

Note how the term *without assistance* is defined as requiring no more than 0.5 calls for assistance a month. This objective can be externally measured and verified.

Example 3: New Security Policy

Here is the desired performance of the new security policy:

> *By following proper labeling and security procedures, employees will not leak confidential material.*

Note the simplicity and clarity of the statement. The desired performance in chapter 3 included more activities than listed here. But activities like labeling information and locking it up are merely a means to the end: no more leaks of confidential material.

Writing Objectives

To achieve the end result—the desired performance—learners must master specific skills. The list of tasks in desired performance compiled in the earlier part of the analysis provides the basis for stating these skills (see chapter 3). This list identifies the main and supporting tasks that the training program must address, and serves as the foundation for writing the objectives of the training program.

Objectives state the skills that learners must master to achieve the end result. Trainers use several terms to refer to objectives: *behavioral objectives, instructional objectives,* and *learning objectives.* The terms are interchangeable, and this book uses all of them.

Each objective has three parts. Figure 4-2 shows the three parts of an objective.

Figure 4-2. The Three Parts of an Instructional Objective

First Part	Second Part	Third Part
State this behavior using an action verb such as *install, type, describe,* and *state.* Avoid words like *know, understand, appreciate,* and *inform* for the behavior because *knowing, understanding,* and *appreciating* (and terms like them) cannot be measured. Usually, each task identified in the needs analysis becomes an objective.	This part describes any issues that should be considered when evaluating the extent to which learners have achieved this objective, such as the availability of reference materials when learners perform the skill. Most frequently, the conditions state whether learners can have access to resources such as a textbook while performing the task.	This describes the extent to which the objective must be achieved to be considered complete, such as "without errors." The level of acceptable performance is assumed to be 100 percent, unless stated otherwise.
↓	↓	↓
"Label all documents classified as confidential with the word *Confidential* in the top margin . . .	. . . using the automatic header and footer function of the word processor . . .	. . . with 100 percent accuracy (both in placing the warning and remembering to use it)."

As noted in Figure 4-2, write all parts of objectives using terms that are both observable and measurable. *Observable* means that a third party—someone not affiliated with the training program—can visibly see evidence that the objective has been achieved. *Measurable* means that a third party can assess the extent to which learners have achieved the specific objectives. The more precisely written the objectives, the more likely that all stakeholders—sponsors, trainers, and learners—will have the same expectations for the program.

The list of objectives usually emerges directly from the list of tasks identified in the needs analysis. If you wrote a task with an observable and measurable action verb, your objective is partly written. Just add conditions and the level of acceptable performance. Also ensure that the action verb states the skill learners must develop as precisely as possible.

In addition, identify any other terms that might be open to several interpretations and reword them as precisely as possible. For example, suppose that the word *effective* is used to indicate the level of acceptable performance. What's effective to one person might not be effective to another. Rather than use the word *effective,* concretely state what constitutes effective performance.

The act of defining abstract words associated with privately held values in an observable and measurable way is called *operationalizing* a term. See Figure 4-3 for examples of effective and ineffective objectives. In the context of the figure, effective means written in the three-part structure using only observable and measurable terms.

Figure 4-3. Effectively and Ineffectively Written Objectives

☒ *Understand the purpose of instructional design.* This is not an example of an objective because it is not observable. You cannot see whether someone "understands" something. Rather, you can observe indicators of understanding, such as describing aspects of the concept and distinguishing one concept from another.

☒ *Know the procedures for installing WordPlus software.* This is not an example of an objective because it is not observable. You cannot see whether someone "knows" something.

☑ *Install WordPlus in five minutes with the use of instructions and without any errors.* This is an example of an objective. It is observable because you can see whether someone could install WordPlus in five minutes or less. It is measurable because you can measure the time needed to install the product and count the number of errors that occurred during installation.

☑ *Name the six key elements of a telecommunications system within 30 seconds and without the assistance of a manual.* This, too, is an example of an objective. The task is "name the six key elements." The conditions are "within 30 seconds" and "without the assistance of a manual." Because the level of performance is not stated, you may assume it is 100 percent.

☑ *Name the six features of WordPlus that distinguish it from other word processors within one minute and without any errors.* This is an example of an objective because the main task can be measured. "Within one minute" is an example of a condition, and "without any errors" indicates the desired level of performance.

Distinguishing Among Main and Supporting Objectives

Just as the tasks serve as the basis for the objectives, so does the hierarchy of the tasks identified earlier serve as the basis of the hierarchy of objectives. At the top of the hierarchy are the most important objectives that learners must master—the main objectives. A training program typically covers between three and seven main objectives. (In the instructional design community, they are called *terminal objectives* because they are the ones that learners must master by the time they end the training program.)

To master one main objective, learners must often master several supporting objectives that help them achieve a main objective. (In the instructional design community, supporting objectives are called *enabling objectives* because they enable a learner to master a main or terminal objective.) To master a supporting objective, learners must sometimes master two or more subsupporting objectives. (Just like the hierarchy of tasks, the hierarchy of objectives can go deeper if needed, such as sub-subsupporting objectives and sub-sub-subsupporting objectives.)

In addition, learners often start a program with the ability to perform certain skills. These are called *entry* or *prerequisite objectives* because they are skills learners acquired before starting the program—and ones they need to succeed in it.

Figure 4-4 is an example of a partial hierarchy of objectives for the course on securing confidential data.

Figure 4-4. Hierarchy of Objectives

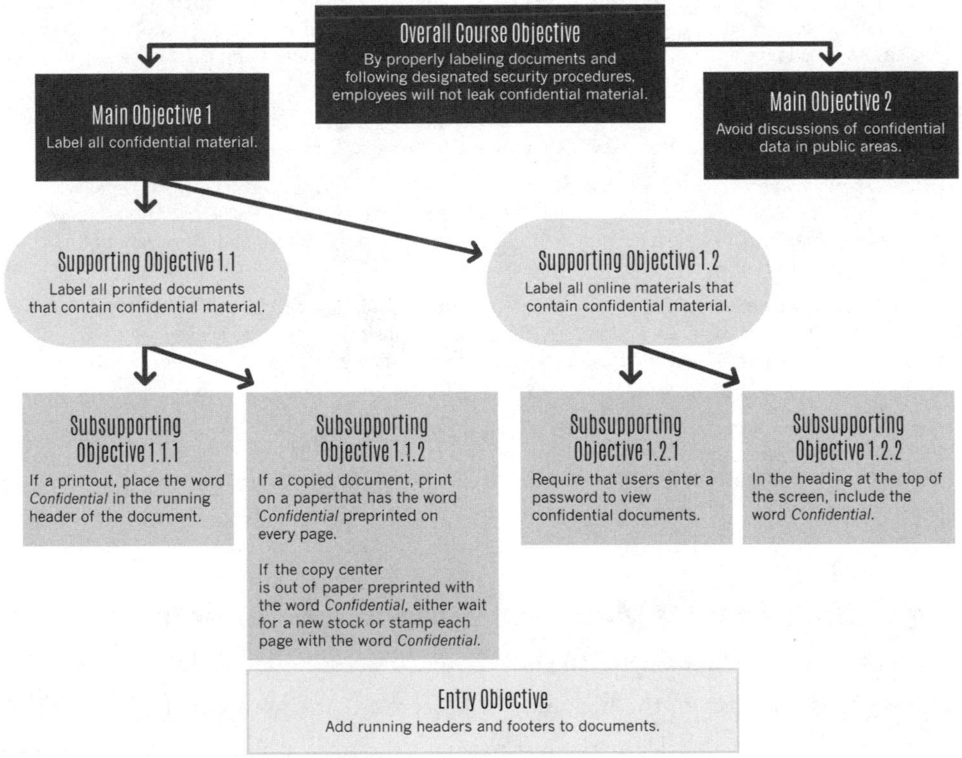

💡 Think About This

In addition to writing instructional objectives, also write business objectives for training programs. A business objective clarifies the business need underlying the program in observable and measurable terms, much as the other instructional objectives clarify the skills to be developed in observable and measurable terms.

When writing a business objective, be sure to include all three parts:

- *Observable, measurable goal:* The goal should focus on one—and only one—of these: "generating" revenue, "reducing or eliminating unnecessary expenses," or "complying with governmental, industry, or corporate regulations."

- *Conditions under which the goal should be achieved:* The date when these business goals should be achieved, such as "within six months" or "by the end of the first quarter."

- *Level of acceptable performance:* For goals pertaining to revenue or expenses, the financial goal, such as "increase by 10 percent," or "reduced to 0.5 percent of sales." For compliance, assume 100 percent unless stated otherwise.

Improving goodwill is not an example of a business objective. It is neither specific nor measurable. Similarly, containing support costs is not an example of a business objective. Which support costs? How much should they be contained? You must be more specific when declaring a business objective.

In contrast, meeting sales projections and reducing help line costs by 10 percent per user are examples of business objectives because they state specifically what types of business benefits should be achieved and how much improvement should occur.

Sponsors often do not seem to notice these business objectives, but write them anyway. They help you focus on the main goal of the project and, more important, suggest to your sponsors how training programs can help them achieve business goals.

Drafting the Evaluations

If the objectives state the goals of the training program, the evaluation materials define what successful achievement of those objectives looks like. For example, if the objective of a training program is "to ensure that no confidential data are leaked by protecting the data," achievement of the objective would involve properly labeling confidential data to ensure that people realize the data's sensitivity and avoid inappropriate disclosure of the data. The evaluation would present learners with data and ask them how they would handle it, checking to see whether learners properly label confidential data and keep it secure.

In other words, the evaluation explores whether learners can apply the skills developed in the program. By designing the evaluation in advance, course designers and developers can "teach to the test"—design courses that focus exclusively on developing the skills addressed in the objectives.

This type of evaluation—intended to be conducted after the training program becomes generally available and that assesses the extent to which the program met its objectives—is called *summative evaluation*. Summative evaluation contrasts with *formative evaluation*, which consists of a series of reviews conducted while developing a training program to determine the likelihood that the program will achieve its objectives. These formative reviews also identify specific parts of the program that might affect success so that trainers can fix them before the program becomes available. One of those parts assessed during the formative evaluation are the summative evaluation materials described in this chapter.

This section explains how to prepare summative evaluations, not formative evaluations. It presents some basic issues underlying evaluation of training programs, and then explains how to prepare three levels of evaluations. (Chapter 9 explains how to plan and conduct formative evaluation activities.)

Basic Issues of Summative Evaluation

Trainers conduct summative evaluations of their training programs to determine the extent to which learners mastered the skills listed in the objectives and to assess the program's effectiveness. Decision makers use the data to inform broader decisions about the training program.

To make sure that summative evaluations provide useful data for informing these decisions, they must assess meaningful issues. Trainers thus rely on criterion-referenced evaluation, in which all test questions and other evaluations of performance are derived from the objectives. The objectives identify the skills worth developing and, by extension, the material worth teaching. As a result, the objectives are the only basis—or criteria—for evaluating the effectiveness of training programs.

Because one type of evaluation at one point in time provides incomplete data, trainers typically rely on several types of summative evaluations. Many trainers use the Kirkpatrick framework to guide development of these summative evaluations. This framework provides a four-level structure for evaluating the actual and perceived effectiveness of training programs (see also Table 1-1 in chapter 1). The different types of evaluation in Kirkpatrick's framework assess participants' reactions to the program (Level 1), how much participants learned (Level 2), the extent to which participants apply the new skills on the job after a period of time (Level 3), and the impact that the training program might have had on the organization that sponsored the program (Level 4). The following sections describe how to prepare Level 1, 2, and 3 evaluations. Level 4 evaluations are beyond the scope of this book. Other books from ATD can help you learn design and conduct evaluations of impact.

Level 1: Assessing Reaction

Almost every classroom course ends with a request for learners to evaluate it. Affectionately known within the industry as smile sheets, these surveys seemingly assess how much participants liked a course, whether the coffee was hot, the food fresh, and the instructor entertaining. E-learning programs end with similar requests. Learners might receive smile sheets right at the end of an online program or within a few days of completing them.

In addition, these surveys can explore participants' reactions to more substantive issues, including:

- whether learners learned anything
- the likelihood that they'll apply the content
- the effectiveness of particular instructional strategies
- the effectiveness of the course "packaging" (such as its structure and the medium used to present it).

The annotated example provided in Figure 4-5 suggests some questions to ask as part of a Level 1 evaluation that can provide meaningful data about the perceived effectiveness of a course.

Level 2: Assessing Learning

To assess the extent to which learners mastered the skills taught in a training program, evaluate their ability to perform the skills immediately after they complete it. Such an assessment pinpoints the specific aspects with which learners have difficulty, so instructors can work with learners to determine why the difficulty exists and how to correct it. The following sections explain how to develop learning assessments, including the source of material for assessments, two popular ways of assessing skills, methods for constructing assessments, and suggestions for preparing feedback to learners.

The Only Valid Source of Material for Assessments

The only appropriate skills to assess are the ones identified in the objectives, regardless of how you choose to assess these skills. Assessments of skills not covered by the objectives are unfair to learners because they go beyond the expectations set with learners at the beginning of a program. If you need to assess a skill not covered by the objectives, revise the list of objectives so it includes the missing skill.

Figure 4-5. Annotated Level 1 Evaluation

Your Opinions, Please

1. In a word, how would you describe this program? _____

Logic behind the question: The question solicits open feedback about the course. It also lets you assess whether students accidentally transposed the numeric scales to subsequent questions (if a student responds "Excellent" to this question, then circles "1" to the next question, chances are the student misread the scales).

2. Using a number, how would you describe this program?

①	②	③	④	⑤
Abysmal		Average		Outstanding

Logic behind the question: The question provides quantitatively oriented organizations with the numbers they seek about the effectiveness of a program.

3. How effectively could you perform <END RESULT> *before* taking this program?

①	②	③	④	⑤
Not at all		Some		A lot

How about *after?*

①	②	③	④	⑤
Not at all		Some		A lot

Logic behind the question: Although this question does not assess actual learning, it does assess perceived learning. That is, do learners perceive that they developed skills through this program, and to what extent?

4. How likely are you to use some or all of the skills taught in this program in your work:

①	②	③	④	⑤
Not at all		Some		A lot

Logic behind the question: The question determines whether learners perceived relevance of the program to their job. Perceived relevance is sometimes correlated with the satisfaction that learners feel with a course.

5. The best part of this program was: _____

_____

_____

6. The one thing that could improve this program most is: _____

_____

_____

Logic behind the question: The last two questions seek qualitative feedback on the program and help prioritize work in a revision. Items mentioned in several responses warrant attention. For example, if 18 learners comment that the pace of the program is slow, fix the pace in the next revision. If one person does not like the colors on the PowerPoint slides, however, it might only be an issue for the individual and probably does not require further attention.

Noted

Ideally, learners would be asked to take the assessment twice: once before starting the training program to identify their entering knowledge level and another immediately afterward. The difference between the "before" and "after" scores is the true measure of learning. Because few organizations require that level of precision, most organizations only conduct the "after" test—a post-test.

Furthermore, write assessments for the main objectives. Because supporting objectives are ones that learners must master to successfully perform the related main objective, assessing the main objective implicitly assesses its supporting objectives as well. When writing assessments of learning, prepare between three and seven questions for each main objective. Although you might only need one question for a test, you can use the remaining questions as activities and exercises in the program.

Two Popular Ways of Assessing Skills

Two popular ways of assessing learning include tests and demonstrations. Tests are written or oral activities performed under an instructor's supervision, who compares the responses provided with the correct responses. When preparing a test, instructors write the questions and state correct responses to each question. For each question they also anticipate two to five incorrect responses that students are likely to give and write feedback to all correct and incorrect responses.

Demonstrations involve learners performing tasks for an instructor, who assesses the match between the manner in which the learner performed the task and the expectations of the instructor. Instructors typically use an observation form to follow the performance, indicating the tasks learners should perform, the order in which learners should perform them, and characteristics to observe in the completed task to assess the extent to which it is correct. A single assessment can integrate both tests and demonstrations, such as the assessment for ATD's Certified Professional in Learning and Performance.

Methods for Constructing Assessments

Constructing test questions begins by developing a question or activity around the action verb in the objective, while incorporating any of the conditions stated in the objective. For example, if the action in the objective is "define," learners should provide a definition. If the action verb in an objective is "use," learners should demonstrate that they can use the equipment, software, or concept. If the action in an objective is "evaluate," learners should provide an evaluation.

Two general classes of questions exist. Objective questions have finite answers and include multiple choice, drag-and-drop, match, and true/false questions. Use them for objectives associated with remembering and comprehending. By contrast, open questions require free-form responses and include short-answer questions, essays, illustrations, and skill demonstrations. Use them for objectives associated with applying, analyzing, evaluating, and creating. Figure 4-6 provides samples of test questions based on specific objectives.

Figure 4-6. Samples of Objectives and Their Related Test Questions

Objective	Sample Test Question
Match the countries with their capitals.	Match the country with its capital: a. France 1. Yaoundé b. Cameroon 2. Brasilia c. Japan 3. Paris d. Thailand 4. Bangkok e. Brazil 5. Tokyo
Name the key steps in the instructional design process according to Dick and Carey.	Name the key steps in the instructional design process, according to Dick and Carey. **[Note that there's no change in wording from the objective.]**
Describe at least three key benefits to small businesses of the X35 copier.	Martin Industries, with 35 employees and $1.2 million in annual revenue, has decided to replace its copiers. Gina Loprieno, office manager, has invited you to make a presentation to the company in an effort to win the business. During the question-and-answer period, Gina comments, "This seems like a great copier but one that's better suited to a company that's much larger than ours. Why should we consider what seems to be more copier than we need?"
Using only the instructions, install the wireless speakers within five minutes and without errors.	You have just received a package containing two new wireless speakers. Install them. You may use the instructions included in the box.
Using effectiveness criteria provided in class, recognize an effectively written performance plan.	On the following pages are samples of three performance plans. Indicate below which of the three are effective, according to the criteria discussed in class.
Given a business case, evaluate the potential opportunity for e-commerce.	Read the following case. Afterward, evaluate the potential opportunity for e-commerce. Specifically name the criteria used in the evaluation.

Suggestions for Preparing Feedback to Learners

Because assessments in most training programs are viewed as tools that help learners develop and sharpen skills, feedback is essential. It provides learners with a general sense of whether they performed correctly or not. If not correct, the feedback suggests which aspects of performance learners need to focus on. To be most effective developmentally, learners receive such feedback after each response. Figure 4-7 suggests a three-part structure for providing meaningful developmental feedback to learners.

Figure 4-7. Three-Part Structure for Providing Meaningful Feedback to Learners

First Part	Second Part	Third Part
Indicate whether the answer is correct or not correct.	In a sentence, explain why the response was correct or not correct.	Tell learners what to do next.
↓	↓	↓
State the feedback with a direct reply. Use the neutral phrase *not correct* rather than more emotionally charged terms like *incorrect* and *wrong* to minimize the emotional response from learners.	State which part of the answer is correct and which part is not, as well as why. To the extent possible, diagnose the source of confusion.	State how learners should proceed, such as "Press Enter to continue" or "Try again." (Only needed for assessments conducted online.)

Level 3: Assessing Transfer to the Job

A training program is successful when learners apply the new skills in their jobs. Therefore, trainers like to assess the extent to which skills transfer into on-the-job behavior after learners have returned to work and a period of time has passed. The amount of time is at the discretion of the trainer, though the earliest that a transfer evaluation should be conducted is four weeks after training and the latest is one year. Ideally, trainers assess transfer at several points over a longer period of time to see not only how much of the training transferred, but also the extent to which learners maintained the change in behavior.

Trainers use a variety of techniques to evaluate transfer. One of the most common is observing the performance of skills covered by the program objectives in the workplace. The observation would ideally use the same forms to observe skill demonstrations that are used to evaluate learning. Another technique is surveying learners and their supervisors. This evaluation method involves asking each learner and the learner's supervisor how well the learner can apply the skills taught in the training program to the job. If both respond that the learner applies skills on the job, the transfer has probably occurred.

Presenting the Analysis and Requirements

After completing the analysis and preparing the requirements, share them with stakeholders. Specifically, share your analysis of the situation, any unique training issues that the sponsors might not have considered, the objectives that need to be achieved, and the evaluations that demonstrate whether learners have achieved these objectives.

Although each organization presents the analysis and requirements in its own way, a general guideline for the write-up is to provide: (1) a brief background on the project (75–100 words) and description of sources of information, (2) a summary of the analysis and findings about the eight issues discussed in chapter 3, and (3) a summary of the requirements (the objectives and evaluations described in this chapter). In some situations, especially when the course designer and developer works for a different employer than the one sponsoring the training program, the course designer and developer shares the report of the analysis and requirements in a brief presentation before presenting the written report.

Stakeholders provide feedback on the report of the analysis and requirements. Typical issues pertain to the business need (usually requiring some slight adjustment to wording); descriptions of performance, tasks, and learners (addressing issues of both clarity and accuracy); and information about constraints (usually identifying a constraint that might have been overlooked). Stakeholders usually request that you adjust the report to reflect the comments received. After revising the report to reflect these comments, ask that the sponsor or a representative officially approve the report, providing you the support needed to proceed with the next phase of the process—design.

Platinum, Silver, and Bronze Types of Projects

The process described in this chapter pertains to a platinum, top-of-the-line training project. But all three types of projects—platinum, silver, and bronze—follow the same process for writing objectives and evaluations. Because writing objectives is so central to the design of evaluations and, later, to the training program, organizations rarely skimp on these tasks. Writing objectives is also a relatively low-cost activity, while offering a high value.

One variation to the process described in this chapter relates to the revisions to existing training programs for silver and bronze projects. Here, sponsors might ask you to limit the work to:

- *Addressing new material:* Write objectives and evaluations that address all new material added to the program.

- *Updating out-of-date objectives and evaluations:* These objectives might refer to outdated processes or products that your organization has replaced; updates replace the outdated information with current material.
- *Adjusting imprecise objectives and related evaluations:* Revisions provide trainers with an opportunity to clarify or make more precise the action verb, conditions, or level of acceptable performance in an objective. Ideally, the training designers find out about these issues before a training program is made available. But when that does not happen, revisions provide an opportunity to address these issues if the sponsor agrees to support them.

Getting It Done

Writing objectives helps focus a training program on developing the identified skills, identifying the relationships among those skills, and determining which skills learners should have before starting this program. Preparing summative evaluations helps maintain that focus, by providing a means for "teaching to the test." Use Exercise 4-1 to guide development of the objectives and summative evaluations for a program. Also try your hand at Exercise 4-2 to test your knowledge of what is a properly written objective.

Exercise 4-1. Developing Objectives and Summative Evaluations

Business objective (optional)	

Instructional objectives	End-result of the program: _____
	Main objective 1: _____
	Supporting objectives:
	  • _____
	  • _____
	  • _____
	  • _____
	  • _____
	
	*Related entry objective (if any):*_____
	
	Main objective 2: _____
	Supporting objectives:
	  • _____
	  • _____
	  • _____
	  • _____
	  • _____
	
	Related entry objective (if any): _____

(continued)

Exercise 4-1. Developing Objectives and Summative Evaluations (continued)

Checking the objectives	Make sure that each objective has: ❑ Observable and measurable behavior ❑ Conditions ❑ Level of acceptable performance (if other than 100 percent)

Evaluation	Have you prepared assessments of:
	• Level 1 (satisfaction)? ❑ Yes ❑ No
	• Level 2 (learning, based on course objectives)?
	  ○ Did you assess all of the main objectives? ❑ Yes ❑ No
	  ○ If needed, did you assess the entry objectives? ❑ Yes ❑ No
	  ○ Do the action verbs in the assessment match those in the objectives?
	   ❑ Yes ❑ No
	  ○ How many questions and activities did you prepare for each objective?____
	  ○ Do you have enough questions or activities for:
	   ○ At least one demonstration question? ❑ Yes ❑ No
	   ○ At least one practice activity? ❑ Yes ❑ No
	   ○ One to assess learning for each version of the test?
	    ❑ Yes ❑ No
	   ○ A follow-up question to verify learning for each version of the test?
	    ❑ Yes ❑ No
	  ○ Did you prepare feedback for each of the questions and activities
	   written? ❑ Yes ❑ No
	• Level 3 (transfer, based on course objectives)?
	  ○ Does the evaluation assess the ability of learners to apply what they
	   learned on the job? ❑ Yes ❑ No
	  ○ Whose views do you solicit (check all that apply)?
	   ❑ Third party ❑ Worker ❑ Supervisor ❑ Co-worker
	  ○ When do you plan to conduct the evaluation (check all that apply)?
	   ❑ 4 weeks ❑ 6 weeks ❑ 2 months
	   ❑ 3 months ❑ 9 months ❑ 12 months

Note: You can also prepare Level 4 evaluations at this time, but a discussion of Level 4 is beyond the scope of this book.

Exercise 4-2. Recognizing Properly Written Objectives

Instructions: For each of the following, indicate whether it is a properly written objective.

1. Know the process for storing information in the cloud.	❑ Yes ❑ No
2. Understand talent development.	❑ Yes ❑ No
3. Name 10 key competencies of talent development professionals.	❑ Yes ❑ No
4. With the assistance of online help, store photos taken on a mobile device in the cloud.	❑ Yes ❑ No

Exercise 4-2. Recognizing Properly Written Objectives (continued)

5. With the assistance of an online policies and procedures guide, authorize tuition reimbursements with 99 percent accuracy (that is, 1 percent or less of authorizations are returned without HR approval).	☐ Yes ☐ No
6. With 80 percent accuracy, the five types of vertebrae in the spine.	☐ Yes ☐ No
7. Understand the key chemicals in the workplace.	☐ Yes ☐ No
8. With the availability of an online manual, employees should complete requests for new mobile telephone accounts using the online request system at 95 percent accuracy (that is, no more than 5 percent of applications rejected by Quality Control).	☐ Yes ☐ No
9. Customer service representatives should accurately update an employee record.	☐ Yes ☐ No

How did you do? Check your answers against these:

1. No. The task "know" is neither observable nor measurable.
2. No. The task "understand" is not observable or measurable. Similarly, the topic "value of talent development" can be interpreted differently by different people, so it can be defined more precisely.
3. Yes. The assumed level of performance is 100 percent. Because no conditions are stated, none are assumed.
4. Yes. The behavior is "store photos taken with a mobile device." The condition is with the assistance of online help. Because it is not stated, the level of acceptable performance is assumed to be 100 percent.
5. Yes. The behavior is authorize and the level of acceptable performance is 99 percent, further clarified as "1 percent or less of authorizations are returned without HR approval."
6. No. No task is stated.
7. No, the task "understand" is not observable or measurable.
8. Yes. The task is "complete request for new mobile telephone accounts using the online request system." The condition is the "availability of an online manual." The level of acceptable performance is stated as "95 percent accuracy (that is, no more than 5 percent of applications rejected by Quality Control)."
9. No. The term *accurately* is too vague and needs to be operationalized—that is, defined in more precisely.

5

The Basics of Organizing Training Programs

 What's Inside This Chapter

This chapter introduces the basics of organizing the instructional material for a classroom or self-study training program. Specifically, it covers:

- Choosing an appropriate format for the training program
- Choosing the communication medium to deliver the training program
- Structuring the training program.

An exercise at the end of this chapter guides you through the process of organizing instructional material for a project on which you are working.

Beginning the Design Process

As noted in chapter 1, design is, in general, a problem-solving process. During analysis, you defined the problem by clarifying the needs underlying the program; describing the learners, learning conditions, and other issues that affect the project; defining the objectives; and preparing the evaluations. Now you are ready for the second activity in the ADDIE approach to designing training programs: design.

This chapter begins a two-chapter sequence that walks you through each of the design decisions that shape the training program. It explains how to choose an appropriate format and communication medium for the training program that addresses the program's objectives, as well as the learning environment and other issues identified in the analysis. This chapter also explains how to structure the program and the units within it and sequence the instructional material. Chapter 6 then explains how to choose an appropriate strategy for teaching the instructional material and how to present the design plans to stakeholders. Later chapters explain how to develop materials from the designs prepared in these two chapters.

 Basic Rule 18

During design, the second activity in ADDIE, you devise a plan for developing a training program that should achieve the objectives with the designated learners and that also addresses the learning conditions and other issues that affect the project.

Designing a training program before developing it offers many benefits. One of the most significant is that it ensures that you have addressed all the objectives in a manner that will successfully develop the intended skills among the intended learners. Design lets you work through enough of the details of the program to make sure that it will work. If the approach does not, you can plan a different approach. Furthermore, working out such issues in design costs less than doing so later in the process. At this point, the training program is just a concept and designers can easily adjust the plans to address particular issues. Later—after you begin developing the program—it contains working parts like scripts, slides, graphics, and videos, and changing them is more costly because the tasks require extensive time and also involve scrapping finished work.

Choosing an Appropriate Format

The first decision in the design phase is the format of the training program. A format for communication material is "a familiar pattern, a way of organizing information that has become so common that readers will probably recognize each new instance as belonging to it" (Price and Price 2002, 272). After providing some background information about formats, this section describes the two most common formats for training programs: live and self-study.

 Basic Rule 19

Your first design task is to identify the format of the training program, as well as the expectations that users bring to it. By identifying the expectations, you can ensure that your designs for the training program explicitly address them.

About Formats

Choosing the right format is important because embedded in the choice is a series of expectations about the material and how it is presented. Take literature, for example. Dramas present people at their most serious; comedies present people at their most humorous; thrillers present mysteries. Dramas that lack tension, comedies that lack humor, and thrillers that seem obvious disappoint readers. In other words, readers bring expectations to different genres of literature.

Similarly, workers bring expectations to training and other informational materials used in the workplace. Workers develop these expectations through repeated exposure to different types of materials. They notice similar characteristics among materials from different sources and, as a result, develop expectations for each type of material. For training and other informational materials, these expectations pertain to:

- *Type of material available:* Different types of training and informational materials present different types of content. A training program develops skills, so it usually presents background concepts and procedures along with explanations of individual steps and demonstrations of a task, and provides learners with opportunities to practice the task and receive feedback. In contrast, a user's guide provides instructions without opportunities to practice. A reference manual provides in-depth explanations without necessarily describing background concepts or procedures for application.
- *Structure or format of the information:* Different types of training and informational materials follow different structures. A training program usually starts with an overview

of the program and logistical information, and closes with a test or assessment and a course evaluation. A user's guide states the purpose of a procedure, lists the materials needed to perform it, then jumps right into the description of the procedure, and ends when the procedure is complete. A reference manual, such as an encyclopedia, follows an alphabetical structure.

- *Writing (communication) style:* Different formats use different communication styles. A training program typically adopts a supportive style. A user's guide might be more direct. A reference manual might present material in a shorthand notation only understood by experts with training.
- *Other expectations:* Additional expectations that learners bring to a format and that designers need to address.

All of these expectations are implicit; workers do not even realize they have them. Furthermore, these expectations are like hygiene; workers notice the absence of something they expect in materials, rather than the presence of an expected characteristic. So designers need to consciously consider these expectations when designing training and informational materials.

The two most common formats for training programs are live and self-study.

Live Training Programs

Live training programs refer to training programs that engage instructors and learners at the same time, such as a face-to-face classroom course, a live webinar, or a virtual class (also called synchronous learning).

Type of material provided: Live training programs usually present background concepts and procedures along with explanations of individual steps and demonstrations of parts or all of the procedures. Live training programs also provide learners with opportunities to practice skills and receive feedback. Activities that learners perform with one another or in discussion with the instructor are also key features of live training programs.

Structure: Live training programs usually begin with a preview of the event as well as logistical information (such as the times of breaks or availability of the instructor outside of class), and then present sequences of instructional material, practice, and feedback in chunks called units. After several units, the program closes with an assessment of learning, information on how to continue learning about the topic, and an evaluation of the learning experience. Sessions of more than 90 minutes include breaks.

Communication style: Live training programs employ clear language, define all new and vague terms, and provide supportive and encouraging messages throughout, especially when providing feedback to learners.

Other expectations: In some instances, learners expect pre-work—some basic material to review before the first formal class session. Learners might also expect to complete assignments between class sessions, and have the scores of their tests reported to their supervisors.

Organizations typically use live training programs to develop interpersonal skills such as handling difficult employee situations; conceptual skills, such as Internet security; behavioral skills, such as physical demonstrations of technical training; and leadership skills.

Self-Study Training Programs

Self-study training programs refer to training programs that learners take at their convenience, such as online tutorials, slidecasts, and printed workbooks (also called asynchronous learning).

Type of material provided: Self-study training programs usually present background concepts and procedures, explanations of procedures, and recorded demonstrations of them, and provide learners with opportunities to practice skills and receive feedback on their performance.

Structure: Self-study training programs usually begin with a preview of the program, and then present completely written or narrated sequences of instructional material. To break up the content as well as verify that learners are synthesizing it, many course designers and developers interject brief questions into the text or recordings. In addition, self-study programs provide learners with exercises to practice the skills presented and offer feedback on performance. As with live training programs, the teaching-and-practice sequences for self-study programs are divided into units. Learners master one unit of content before proceeding to the next. After several units, the program closes with an assessment of learning and information on how to continue learning about the topic. In some instances, learners are also asked to complete and return an evaluation of the learning experience.

Communication style: Self-study training programs are thoroughly scripted. Course designers write each word of the instructional material. All activities are scripted to anticipate both correct and incorrect responses by learners and offer appropriate feedback for both. When scripting, course designers and developers employ clear language, define all new and vague terms, and provide supportive and encouraging messages throughout, especially when providing feedback to learners.

Other expectations: Learners expect self-study training programs to be self-contained—that is, the program materials provide everything learners need. If learners need to consult other sources, such as textbooks or websites, the program materials should direct learners to those materials and state when to return to the program materials.

Organizations typically use self-study training programs to develop fundamental skills, such as basic policies and procedures, and foundational knowledge, such as names and facts about products. Organizations also use self-study training programs to teach software applications and for compliance training (training required by a government agency, industry group, or top leadership of the organization).

Choosing a Communication Medium

The next decision in the design phase is the medium used to deliver the training program to learners. So far, the discussion in this book has not considered whether the training program is intended to be delivered face-to-face, online, or in print. That's because you should analyze the needs underlying a program, write objectives, and develop draft evaluations before deciding how the material will be presented. Furthermore, you should choose the most appropriate format for the content before determining how to deliver it, as most formats can be delivered in several media. For example, a live class can be delivered face-to-face in a classroom or similar facility, or online as a live virtual class or webinar. Similarly, a tutorial can be presented online or in a workbook.

 Basic Rule 20

The second design task is to identify the medium of the training program, as well as its advantages and disadvantages. By identifying these, you can ensure that your designs for the training program take advantage of the advantages and minimize the disadvantages.

The communication medium used to deliver the training program is significant because it has an effect on the structure of the program and the presentation of instructional material. Learners might also need access to playback equipment and other technical features to use some media.

Course designers and developers typically choose among three media to deliver training programs: face-to-face, online, and print.

Face-to-Face

The first—and most traditional—communication medium to deliver training programs is the face-to-face (physical) classroom. Face-to-face programs can occur in classrooms specifically designed for the purpose; meeting rooms that serve a number of purposes; or alternative settings, such as a table in a coffee shop.

Trainers typically deliver longer programs face-to-face. They also choose this medium when relationships are essential to the learning experience, such as with management and leadership programs; when learners must physically demonstrate skills, such as with certain types of technical training; when the total number of learners is limited; and when design and development time is limited (other media require more time to develop than face-to-face training programs). Table 5-1 lists some advantages and disadvantages of face-to-face programs.

Table 5-1. Advantages and Disadvantages of Face-to-Face Programs

Advantages	Disadvantages
It is among the easiest to develop, minimizing development time and costs.	It is the most expensive to deliver because learners must leave their workplace to take training. Often, learners must travel, adding airfare, lodging, meals, and related expenses to the total cost of the program. If learners do not need to travel, the instructor might. Additional expenses include rental or purchase of classroom facilities, equipment, and supplies for learners.
When teaching, an instructor can easily adjust the instructional material to the needs of learners. If an instructor sees a puzzled look, the instructor can respond with a clarification. If a learner has a question, she can immediately ask it.	Material is often presented inconsistently between class sessions because the instructor might adjust the material to the personality of each class. The instructor might use different words to explain a concept, introducing subtle differences in meanings, or cover material in one class session but not another.
Under the watchful eye of the instructor, a large percentage of learners complete the program.	Learners must take the program when the instructor offers it, which might be inconvenient for learners.
Updating the training program is easy because it usually just requires a quick change of a slide or two, perhaps an update to an activity, and a change to the notes.	With poor design, classroom sessions can degenerate into lectures, bore learners to sleep, and fail to achieve the objectives.
Classrooms comfort all stakeholders. Learners and instructors appreciate the face-to-face visibility and the ease with which it facilitates relationship building. Instructors, managers, and sponsors appreciate the accountability of seeing which learners attend class sessions.	

Online

The second, and increasingly common, communication medium used to deliver training programs is online. According to recent *ATD State of the Industry* reports, organizations use online technology to delivery nearly 40 percent of all training. Learners take online programs on desktop and laptop computers, tablets (like an iPad or Microsoft Surface), and smartphones (like an iPhone or Android phone).

The programs could be live, when learners and the instructor are online at the same time, sometimes called *synchronous online learning* or the *live virtual classroom*. Typically, synchronous online training programs let learners and the instructor communicate with one another, and let the instructor show slides, mark up the slides, and ask a variety of types of questions of learners. The instructor might ask learners to respond to the questions by typing or speaking through their microphones. Many live virtual classroom applications let the instructor divide learners into groups and work within their groups, even when the learners are in different locations.

Online programs can also be recorded for use when learners and instructors are not online at the same time, called *asynchronous online learning*. Typically, asynchronous online programs are self-study, and learners take them at their own pace and at a convenient time. Most self-study programs include activities and evaluations, and can provide feedback to learners based on their responses. When learners need to interact with the instructor, they do so by sending an email or text message, or calling the instructor, and thus might not receive an immediate response.

Table 5-2 summarizes the advantages and disadvantages of online training programs.

Table 5-2. Advantages and Disadvantages of Online Training Programs

Online Training Program	Advantages	Disadvantages
Synchronous programs (live virtual classes)	Instructors can relatively easily adjust the instructional material to the needs of the learners. If instructors receive feedback from learners in the class session that they do not understand the material, instructors can clarify it. If learners have questions, they can immediately ask them.	Learners must have access to appropriate equipment and a reliable, uninterrupted Internet connection to participate in the event.
	Organizations avoid class-related travel costs because, as long as they have reliable Internet connections, learners and instructors can participate in a program from their home locations.	Design and development of live virtual classes requires slightly more time than for face-to-face classes because interactions must be planned more thoroughly and instructors require rehearsals for the first several class sessions.

Table 5-2. Advantages and Disadvantages of Online Training Programs (continued)

Online Training Program	Advantages	Disadvantages
Synchronous programs (live virtual classes)	To compensate for the mediated communication between learners and instructors, course designers and developers more extensively think through the design of instruction and pay more attention to fostering interaction between learners and instructors.	Because it is mediated, communication between learners and instructors can sometimes feel awkward and less spontaneous than face-to-face.
	Updating the training program is easy because it usually just requires a quick change of a slide or two, perhaps an update to an activity, and a change to the notes.	Instructors need special training on the complex software used to teach online. Some instructors might also require an assistant nearby throughout the first few webcasts.
	Learners who might not participate much in a face-to-face class often feel more comfortable participating in the slightly more anonymous virtual classes.	Various technical issues can arise. Software used for the virtual classroom might lack the capabilities instructors need. Learners might prefer to take courses on tablets and smartphones but the software might not permit it. Technical difficulties can arise during class.
		At their worst, online classes involve endless lectures that require little to no interaction. Learners multitask, answering email and reading the news during the webcast, reducing the likelihood that they will achieve the intended objectives.
Asynchronous programs (tutorials)	Learners can take programs whenever they need them, as long as they have a access to a copy of the program.	Learners must have access to equipment to view the materials, as well as a reliable Internet connection.
	Because learners can take programs at their own convenience, employers avoid travel-to-training expenses.	Design and development of asynchronous training programs requires at least twice as much time as live programs, because all materials must be thought through and recorded in advance. The most highly interactive courses require more than 10 times more time to design and develop than live programs.

(continued)

Table 5-2. Advantages and Disadvantages of Online Training Programs (continued)

Online Training Program	Advantages	Disadvantages
Asynchronous programs (tutorials)	Material is taught consistently because all learners use the same recordings of the material. This ensures that learners hear the same concepts using the same terms and without subtle differences in meanings.	Design and development costs are similarly more expensive; organizations realize the savings in delivery costs.
	Courses can employ a variety of media, including videos, audio sequences, text, visuals, games, and links to related websites.	Course designers and developers require training on the complex software used to create online materials.
	To compensate for the lack of direct interaction between learners and the instructor, course designers and developers more extensively think through the design of instruction and pay more attention to clarity and usability than live training programs.	Updating asynchronous courses can be challenging, especially updating video and audio recordings, because revisions require some re-recording that can also introduce inconsistencies.
	Because computers can process information, course designers and developers can tailor courses to specific learning needs and provide remediation (review and tutoring) when learners have difficulty with the material without embarrassing learners who need it or annoying learners who do not.	If they have questions, learners do not have immediate access to an instructor.
		Technical issues can arise while learners take the programs. Software used for creating the courses might lack the capabilities course designers seek. Learners might prefer to take courses on tablets and smartphones but the software might not permit it.
		At their worst, online tutorials involve endless recordings of boring presentations that involve little to no interaction, reducing the likelihood that learners will achieve the intended objectives.

Trainers typically deliver online training programs for shorter courses. They also use online programs when relationships are less essential to the learning experience, such as policy and procedure training and some technical training; when the learners apply the skills taught in class online, such as software training; and for training programs that must be available on demand, such as compliance training; and when large numbers of people must receive training.

Print

The third, and least common, communication medium used to deliver training programs is print. Course designers and developers use print in two instances: to prepare supporting materials for classroom courses, such as student handouts and exercises, and to prepare self-study workbooks.

Table 5-3 offers some advantages and disadvantages of printed materials.

Table 5-3. Advantages and Disadvantages of Printed Materials

Advantages	Disadvantages
Because printed materials require no equipment to read or view them, learners can take them anywhere.	Organizations need to develop policies on which materials they print for learners and which materials they expect learners to print themselves.
Although printed materials require no equipment to read or view, PDF and similar formats of printed materials let learners view them on an electronic device.	When organizations expect learners to print their own materials, learners must have access to a computer, an Internet connection, and a printer. If learners do not have a printer, they can often view the materials anyway, but must have a portable device on which to do so.
Learners of all ages are familiar—and comfortable—with printed materials.	Other than printing and shipping costs (if organizations print materials), the cost to deliver self-study workbook training programs is minimal because learners can take them wherever they want.
Moderate design and development time. Because course designers and developers expect learners to read printed materials on their own, they must think through the presentation, clarity, and usability of material in advance just as they do for asynchronous online materials. But because development is less complex than asynchronous online materials, less design and development time is needed.	If organizations want to make print materials available for reading online using e-book readers like the Kindle and iPad, they must also determine which e-book formats to use and add time to the schedule for each format in which they produce materials.
Moderate design and development costs. Because print requires less design and development time, it also costs less.	Updating printed materials can be challenging, especially if the organization prints and stores materials. Revising outdates all printed materials, so trainers must scrap them.
	Even when instructors expect learners to print materials for a live class, learners do not always do so.

(continued)

Table 5-3. Advantages and Disadvantages of Printed Materials (continued)

Advantages	Disadvantages
	If learners using self-study printed materials have questions, they do not have immediate access to the instructor.
	At their worst, printed self-study materials are merely a book, not a workbook: endless narrative with little opportunity to practice, reducing the likelihood that students will achieve the intended objectives.

 Think About This

Although the original request to design and develop a training program might have identified a preferred medium, when choosing a medium, you also verify that the medium requested is the most appropriate for achieving the program's objectives while addressing some of the other practical issues identified in the needs assessment. If the preferred medium is not the most appropriate, suggest your recommended medium to the sponsor along with an explanation for the change.

Structuring the Training Program

Once you've selected the format and communication medium, you can turn your attention to the third task in the design phase: structuring the training program. Structure plays a crucial role in the design of effective training because it involves formally establishing a program, clearly sequencing the material so learners can easily link one point to the next, and dividing the instructional material into manageable chunks or units so that learners are asked to master only as much material as they can process at one time. What follows are the key tasks in structuring a training program.

 Basic Rule 21

Structuring a training program involves (1) establishing a general structure for the program, (2) developing a general structure for each unit, (3) sequencing the instructional material, (4) breaking the instructional material into units, (5) planning for the needs of learners, and (6) representing the structure with an information map.

1. Establish a General Structure for the Training Program

Every live and self-study training program follows a certain general structure, regardless of the format, medium, or instructional material. Each begins with certain elements (called *front matter*) and ends with other elements (called *back matter*). Although front and back matter are supposed to appear in every training program, unless you specifically plan for them, you might forget to include them. Therefore, your first task in organizing the training program is establishing the general structure and making sure you include all of the front and back matter.

Front and Back Matter for a Live Training Program

In a live training program, the instructor presents much of the front matter to learners. The front matter includes:

- Title page or screen, which includes the program's title, its number or identifier (such as HR-1544), the instructor's name, the instructor's department and organization (such as Training Department or Acme Corporation), and a copyright notice if needed (such as © Copyright. Association for Talent Development. 2015. All rights reserved).

- Purpose of training program, which states the desired end result, usually copied from the analysis performed earlier.

- Agenda or objectives. The agenda is a list of the topics covered by the training program. The objectives are the main objectives of the course (only list supporting objectives in the units in which they are taught). Some organizations use an agenda, some use the objectives, and some use both.

- Prerequisites (if any), which lists skills learners must already have mastered to successfully complete the program.

- Administrivia, which refers to logistical information that orients learners to the classroom schedule and facilities. For face-to-face programs, administrivia includes the time of breaks and meals; location of meals and breaks if they are provided, or restaurant suggestions if meals are not provided; the location of restrooms; emergency number, where learners can be reached in case of an emergency; the location of emergency exits; a request to turn off mobile phones; and other material, as suggested by your organization. For live virtual programs, administrivia also includes instructions—and ideally practice—for communicating with the instructor during the webcast; instructions on how to proceed if learners lose their connection to the webcast; telephone number of someone outside of the class whom learners can contact if a technical problem arises during the webcast; a request to mute microphones and avoid multitasking; and other material, as suggested by your organization.

The back matter for a live program includes six items. First, a summary of the key points in the instructional material. Second, a test or assessment (if offered). Third, a list of related training programs and other resources. Fourth, information on how to receive follow-up support, such as websites with additional exercises and material, number for telephone support, and address for email support, if that is available. Fifth, a program evaluation (and if offered, information about a follow-up Level 3 evaluation to be conducted several weeks or months after the course). And sixth, the certificate of completion if offered (or information about how learners will receive it if provided after class).

Front and Back Matter for a Self-Study Program

In a self-study training program, learners read or view the front and back matter on their own. As a result, it must be sufficiently clear that learners can understand it without assistance. The front matter for a self-study training program includes:

- Title page or screen, which includes the program's title, its number or identifier, the instructor's name, the instructor's department and organization, and the date that the program was most recently updated.
- Edition notice, which contains legal notices, including the copyright notice. The edition notice also contains a list of trademarks, registered trademarks, and service marks used in the program.
- Preface, which learners read to determine whether they should take the training program. It describes the purpose of program, which states the desired end result, taken directly from the analysis phase; the main objectives (only list supporting objectives in the units in which they are taught); and intended audience, which explicitly states the learners for whom the program is intended.
- Prerequisites (if any), which lists skills learners must have already mastered to successfully complete the program. In some instances, the preface might refer to an assessment learners can take to determine whether they have the prerequisite skills. Online programs might link to the assessment.
- Instructions, which describe how to take the program, explain unique symbols used in the program, and provide other information that might require an explanation before learners can effectively use the program.

The back matter for a self-study training program includes six items. First, a summary of the key points of the instructional material. Second, a glossary of terms used in the program. Third, a test or assessment if offered. Fourth, a list of related training programs and other resources. Fifth, a program evaluation (and if offered, information about a follow-up Level 3 evaluation to be conducted several weeks or months after the program). And sixth, information on how to receive a certificate of completion if one is offered.

 **Noted**

Many organizations have their own lists of items for the front and back matter (as well as instructions on how to prepare them). Before proceeding, check with your project manager to find out whether your organization has standard front and back matter.

Organizations that have their own lists of items for front and back matter often have *templates*, which are forms that you can easily fill in to create this material. These templates not only simplify your work, but also ensure consistency across training programs. If all course designers and developers use the same template for a preface in a workbook, for example, learners know where to find the information they need to determine whether a self-study program meets their needs.

2. Develop a General Structure for Each Unit

Each unit in a program also has its own front and back matter. Like the front and back matter for a training program, it is possible to overlook the front and back matter for a unit if you do not take a few moments to explicitly identify it.

For live training programs and self-study programs, the front matter for a unit might include a new unit slide (which indicates the title of the unit and its sequence number), the objectives of the unit, and the prerequisites for the unit. When listing the objective, state the main and supporting objectives covered. Do not cover sub-supporting objectives and objectives lower in the hierarchy as this would confuse learners. The list of prerequisites also indicates where

 **Noted**

Units are also often referred to as lessons and sections. Use whichever term you prefer, so long as you use it consistently throughout the program.

learners can find this material (such as another unit or course), and might include a pretest to help learners determine whether they already have these skills. The back matter might include a summary, an assessment of learning, a list of other resources about the topic, and job aids that help learners apply the skills taught in the unit back on the job.

3. Sequence the Instructional Material

The next task in structuring the course is to determine how to sequence the instructional material. One large chunk of this task is already finished: determining what to cover. Only include material that directly relates to the learning objectives in the training program. These objectives state which skills the program should develop and the hierarchy of skills (main objectives, supporting objectives, subsupporting objectives). Trainers call this criterion-referenced instruction, because all instructional material emerges from the learning objectives or (criteria).

In this task, you determine in which order to present these objectives to learners. Take time to sequence the objectives so that the order is readily apparent to anyone who looks at the program. The clearer the sequence of the content, the easier a time learners will have acquiring individual skills and linking them together to achieve the end result. This is especially true for self-study courses, which learners take at their own pace and without assistance.

In his influential book *Information Anxiety*, information architect Richard Saul Wurman (1989) suggests five general schemes for sequencing content or, as he calls them, hat racks. Wurman's five hat racks are:

- category
- time
- location
- alphabet
- continuum.

You can develop complementary, though different, sequences at each level of the hierarchy of the training program. That is, you can develop one sequence for the overall course that sequences all the main objectives. Then you might develop separate organizational schemes within the discussions of each main objective.

For example, suppose you are developing a self-study training program on information security. The overall training program might be organized by a time sequence, from preventing a security leak to discovery of a security leak to addressing that security leak. But you might sequence individual objectives differently. The first unit of the program might identify the different categories of security leaks. These might be treated as an alphabet, presenting categories in alphabetical order. The second unit might address procedures for securing information. This might be presented as a time sequence, from start to finish. And the third unit might explore the discovery of security leaks, and include a list of security leaks and their severity. These might be presented in a continuum, from most to least serious.

4. Break the Instructional Material Into Units

After sequencing all of the instructional material (which might require several layers of organization), break the material into smaller packages—the units. This makes the material manageable for learners and helps control the amount of information that learners must consider at any given time. As noted in chapter 1, adult learners have a limited attention span because they are pressed for time and because they have a finite capacity for learning content at one time.

Although some would characterize the act of dividing the content into units as a science, it is really an art, during which, in some cases, you have to rely on gut feelings when determining how much content to put into a unit.

 Think About This

Wondering how to divide content into individual units? A typical unit should last one to two hours to match the attention spans of learners. Consider these guidelines for reaching that point:

- For a classroom course, a unit should last about 50–90 minutes (which, one experienced trainer said, is the longest a person can go between bio-breaks).
- For a workbook course, a unit should last no longer than 30–60 minutes.
- In practical terms, each unit typically addresses one main objective. In the case of an extremely complex course, you might only cover one supporting objective in a unit.
- If a unit goes on longer than one to two hours, consider dividing it into separate parts.

5. Plan for the Needs of Learners

Some learners will not grasp the material on the first try, other learners will apply the material in a unique way, and still others will want to learn more about the topic. The best way to address learners' needs is to design with all of them in mind. So after developing the overall structure for the program, sequencing the instructional content, and dividing it into units, plan for three special needs of learners: remediation, special application of the material, and enrichment.

Remediation

Some learners might need more assistance in learning than others. Some might not comprehend the material on the first try and thus need to review it. Others might think they correctly understand the material but their performance on activities and assessments suggests otherwise. This type of review—with the hope of correcting learning errors—is called remediation.

When designing for remediation, anticipate material that learners might have difficulty grasping and the points in the learning process during which the learners' difficulties become visible, such as during an activity or after a quiz—times when learners need to demonstrate their new skills. Then determine how to provide the remediation.

Some course designers and developers have learners go through the instructional material a second time. But that's not necessarily helpful. If learners did not grasp an explanation as written the first time, they are less likely to grasp it after a second reading. More appropriate is preparing an alternate presentation of the content, which assumes that learners know less than was assumed in the initial presentation. It should also make use of other instructional approaches, such as visual ones (if the initial presentation relied primarily on text).

Special Applications of the Material

Sometimes, you need to tailor instructional material to address unique issues that arise in work environments. Suppose that 30 percent of learners taking the course on the corporate security policy work with especially sensitive material about new product information, whereas another 20 percent work with sensitive personnel data. Although both types of information are confidential, the reasons for keeping the material confidential, the means of protecting it, and the liabilities for disclosing it differ.

In such situations, you can help learners make more effective use of the learning material by describing how they can apply the material in their work environments. To do so, you would customize passages in those parts of the program to describe issues that arise in particular environments. For example, in the unit about disclosing confidential material in public places, you might have two separate examples: one about the effects of sharing confidential product news, and another about sharing the particulars of an employee's family situation that is affecting his or her work performance.

Enrichment

Some learners might want to learn more about the material after completing a unit or training program. If later units do not cover the additional material, you might support enthusiasm by linking learners to enrichment material.

Needs for enrichment vary, depending on the material and the learners. In some cases, enrichment might involve exercises that take learners beyond the material presented in the training program. In other cases, enrichment might be a list of resources to help learners continue their learning, such as related learning programs (online and in the classroom), links to related websites, and a list of references.

6. Represent the Structure With an Information Map

After devising the structure for the learning program, record it. Although most people are trained to use outlines to represent the structure of a training program, consider using information maps instead, in which the structure is more visible and easier to follow. An information map diagrams the overall structure of a training program and diagrams how the material relates to one another.

Generally, an information map has major and minor nodes. Major nodes represent main sections or units of a training program; minor nodes represent subsections or lessons. Figure 5-1 is an example of an information map for the program on corporate security. (Note that this information map only covers supporting objectives, not subsupporting objectives.)

Figure 5-1. Information Map

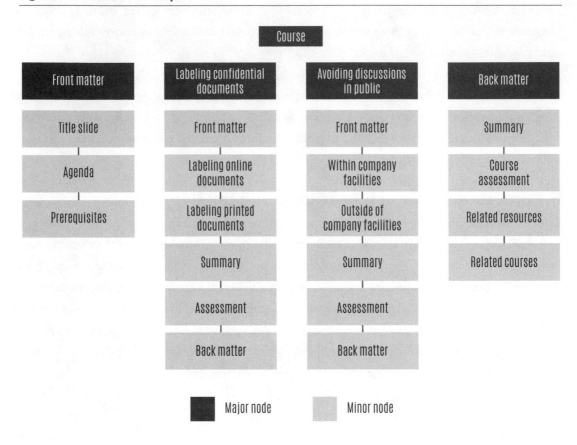

Platinum, Silver, and Bronze Types of Projects

The process for organizing training programs described in this chapter assumes that you work on a platinum—high visibility and profile—project.

For silver—moderate visibility and profile—and bronze—low visibility and profile—projects, the general process remains the same. However, cost and development time affect the design choices made by course designers and developers. Organizations increasingly choose online self-study tutorials for both silver and bronze projects. Although design and development costs for online self-study tutorials exceed those of face-to-face live training programs, they have significantly lower delivery costs. Furthermore, learners can take online self-study training programs whenever needed, instead of when a class is scheduled.

With limited time to develop programs, many course designers and developers turn to the live virtual classroom. These programs require less development time than tutorials and have lower delivery costs because no one must travel to training, and the instructor can record the program, so the recording is available as self-study material later. This is especially useful for bronze projects.

Whenever possible—especially with bronze projects—organizations encourage course designers and developers to reuse existing materials when designing new programs. For example, say an organization wants a new program that addresses time management, but the organization already has an existing program with a time management unit. Course designers and developers might incorporate that unit into the new program. Similarly, if a new program explains how to install a piece of equipment, the course designer and developer might integrate the installation procedure from the user's guide rather than writing a new procedure.

Because many silver and bronze projects are revisions to existing programs, designers might skip some decision-making steps, like the format and medium, because those decisions were made previously. Furthermore, when structuring material, designers must work with the existing overall structure for the program and integrate new material where it fits within the existing scheme. A major reorganization would essentially result in a new program and significantly change the scope.

In both instances of using existing material—reuse and revision—course designers try to make the old and new material appear as similar as possible. To ensure that happens, course designers and developers might begin the process by creating an information map of the existing material and its structure, and noting the choices made. The better designers understand how previous designers made decisions about a program's structure, the more consistent the decisions of the current designers will appear to learners.

Getting It Done

The first two tasks in design include choosing the format for your training program (live or self-study training program) and choosing the communication medium (face-to-face, online, or print). The next task is structuring the program: establishing a general structure for the program, developing a general structure for each unit, sequencing the instructional material, dividing the instructional material into units, planning for the needs of learners, and representing the structure with an information map.

Use Exercise 5-1 to guide these design tasks for a program you are developing. After you have chosen a format and a communication medium for the training program and organized the structure, you can start thinking about how to present the material.

Exercise 5-1. Organizing the Content of Your Training Program

Choosing a format for the training program	☐ Live ☐ Self-study	For selected format, identify: ☐ Type of material ☐ Structure of information ☐ Communication style ☐ Other expectations
Choosing a communication medium for the program	☐ Face-to-face ☐ Online ☐ Print Who prints? __ Learner? __ Your organization?	For selected medium, identify: ☐ Advantages ☐ Disadvantagess

Exercise 5-1. Organizing the Content of Your Training Program (continued)

Establishing a general structure for your program	Live training program	Self-study training program
	Front matter	*Front matter*
	❑ Title slide:	❑ Title page or screen:
	__ Title of the program	__ Title of the program
	__ Number or identifier of the program	__ Number or identifier of the program
	__ Instructor's name	__ Instructor's name
	__ Instructor's department and organization	__ Instructor's department and organization
	❑ Purpose	❑ Edition notice:
	❑ One of the following:	__ Copyright notice
	__ Agenda	__ List of trademarks
	__ Objectives (main only)	❑ Preface
	❑ Prerequisite skills (if any)	__ Purpose
	❑ Administrivia:	__ Objectives (main only)
	__ Face-to-face: times of breaks and meals, locations or suggestions for meals; locations of restrooms; emergency number; emergency exits; request to turn off mobile phones; other material suggested by your organization	__ Intended audience
		__ Prerequisites (state as skills, not just names of courses)
		__ Instructions for taking the course
		Back matter
		❑ Summary
		❑ Glossary
		❑ Test or assessment (if offered)
		❑ List of related courses and other resources
	__ Live virtual: instructions for communicating with the instructor during the webcast; instructions on how to proceed in a lost connection; telephone number for technical problems; a request to mute microphones and avoid multitasking; other material, as suggested by your organization	❑ Program evaluation
		❑ Certificate of completion (if offered)
	Back matter	
	❑ Summary	
	❑ Test or assessment (if offered)	
	❑ List of related programs and other resources	
	❑ Follow-up support	
	❑ Program evaluation	
	❑ Certificates of completion	

(continued)

Exercise 5-1. Organizing the Content of Your Training Program (continued)

Setting up a general structure for each unit	Live training program *Front matter* ❑ New unit slide ❑ Objectives (the main and supporting objectives for the unit) *Back matter* ❑ Summary ❑ Assessment (such as a quiz or test) ❑ Resources ❑ Job aids	Self-study training program *Front matter* ❑ Title page for the unit ❑ Objectives (the main and supporting objectives for the unit) ❑ Prerequisites for the unit (stated as skills) *Back matter* ❑ Summary ❑ Assessment of learning ❑ Resources ❑ Job aids
Developing a structure for specific learning content	❑ Overall structure of the course: __ Category __ Time __ Location __ Alphabet __ Continuum ❑ Structure for main objective 1: __ Category __ Time __ Location __ Alphabet __ Continuum **[Repeat for each main objective of the program]**	
Dividing the content into units	Live training program Units should range from 50 to 90 minutes	Self-study training program Units should range from 30 to 50 minutes
Planning for remediation and enrichment	• Plans for remediation: _____ _____ • Plans for special application of the content: _____ _____ • Plans for enrichment: _____	
Representing the structure with an information map		

6

The Basics of Choosing
an Instructional Strategy

 ## What's Inside This Chapter

This chapter introduces the most common techniques for presenting instructional material in training programs and helps you start to build your repertoire of training design techniques. It opens with a discussion of the characteristics of an engaging training program, explaining why effective training involves more than imparting facts. Next, it presents some common means for engaging learners—called instructional strategies—and explains when to use them:

- classical approach
- mastery learning
- discovery learning
- performance without instruction.

The chapter closes with a discussion of how to choose among these instructional strategies and how to present your design plans to sponsors.

An exercise at the end of this chapter provides a framework for presenting design plans for a project on which you are working to stakeholders.

This chapter concludes a two-chapter sequence on the design of training program. Chapter 5 explained how to make the first several decisions in the design process, including choosing a format for your training program (such as live or self-study program), choosing the communication medium (such as face-to-face, online, or print), and structuring the program.

This chapter explains how to choose an instructional strategy which presents material to learners in a way that they will likely develop and retain the intended skills. It also explains how to formally present the design plans to sponsors for their approval before you proceed with the costly process of developing the program. But before you can choose the instructional strategy, you need to become familiar with the characteristics of an engaging training program.

Characteristics of an Engaging Training Program

For some course designers and developers, choosing a strategy for presenting the instructional material to learners is the most creative design choice. You get to choose among many approaches to presenting, reinforcing, and practicing the content. In some cases, the material might dictate the approach. In others, several workable strategies might exist and you need to decide which one best fits with the particular set of learners, instructors, and conditions of a project.

The instructional strategy should motivate learners to find meaning in the material, develop the skills taught, and apply them on the job. In other words, the choice of an instructional strategy provides the foundation for a motivating, active, and supportive learning experience. When learners want to learn and believe that they can succeed, they're more likely to do so.

 Basic Rule 22

> To ensure that learners want to learn and that the learning sticks, choose an instructional strategy that creates a motivating, active, and supportive learning experience.

A Motivating Learning Experience

Before learners can master the instructional material, they often first need to become motivated to learn. Learners are motivated by two general issues.

The first is relevance: the subject of the training program must seem relevant to the learner. Immediate relevance to the job or to longer-term career plans tends to motivate learners. General interest in the subject also motivates learners.

The second is the belief among learners that they can successfully learn the material. Called *self-efficacy*, this concept focuses on learners' beliefs about their ability to learn, not their actual capacity to learn, because the belief alone often affects the capacity.

Noted

What makes training motivating? For some learners, certain material is intrinsically interesting. For others, successfully mastering the content is essential to success in a new job or offers the possibility of career advancement, such as a new job assignment, certification, or promotion.

But for others, learning new materials requires that they unlearn what they already know. Rather than motivate, this serves as a barrier to learning. As one designer for software trainer commented:

> *"Our learners often wonder why they have to learn a new system. They were satisfied with the old one. Management bought a new one without asking. The learners don't want to switch systems, much less learn the new one."*

In these cases, course designers and developers must address this motivational barrier so learning can begin. The more you uncover about learners in the needs assessment, the better you can identify the motivators and barriers to learning and address them in your course designs.

An Active Learning Experience

Learners learn best when they are actively involved in the learning experience. So course designers and developers integrate activities into training programs that engage people in the learning process such as exercises, case studies, discussions, and games. In fact, some organizations require that a certain percentage of programs (say, a third of all material) involves active learning.

When integrating activities, course designers and developers need to make clear the relevance of the activities to achieving the objectives. At the beginning of a unit, for example, activities might spark interest in the instructional material or address prior knowledge. During a unit, activities might provide learners with opportunities to verify their knowledge and apply the skills taught.

Avoid gratuitous activities that engage learners but have no relationship to the instructional material. Although fun, these activities also deliver a subtle, negative message: "This is the fun stuff. When it is over, we need to return to the boring instructional material."

A Supportive Learning Experience

Learners learn best when they feel good about the learning experience. Therefore, course designers and developers design learning to enhance learners' belief in and feelings of success. To maintain a supportive learning environment, avoid overwhelming and embarrassing the learners.

To avoid overwhelming learners, simplify the content. For example, if seven ways exist to perform a particular task, present just one. By mastering one, learners feel success. Hearing about all seven, learners may feel confused and struggle to master any of them.

To avoid embarrassing learners, start with simple exercises and work to more complex ones, so that learners build comfort with the easy-to-master material before handling the more challenging scenarios. Similarly, only test content that directly relates to the objectives and that has already been taught to ensure that learners are prepared for assessments.

Four Common Instructional Strategies for Presenting Material

Instructional strategies suggest how to introduce the material to learners, how to present the material, how to reinforce and practice the skills taught, and how to conclude the presentation of the material. A typical training program has a general instructional strategy for the entire program, as well as specific strategies for each unit.

Several instructional strategies exist, each motivating, involving, and supporting learners in a unique way. Some strategies involve more interactivity; others convey content more efficiently. Some are inexpensive to develop but involve limited interaction; others require more resources but display more creativity. Some strategies work more easily in certain media than others.

Basic Rule 23

Consider a variety of strategies for presenting content before making a decision on a particular one to use in a given situation.

No one strategy fits all learning situations. Each offers advantages and disadvantages for building the intended skills. When choosing among the strategies, consider how the advantages and disadvantages of a given strategy affect your particular learning situation.

The four most common instructional strategies used by course designers and developers are the classical approach, mastery learning, discovery learning, and performance without instruction. The next sections separately discuss each strategy and offer suggestions for choosing an appropriate one for a given training program. (Note that this discussion mentions instructors. When doing so, this discussion assumes that the instructor for the course is someone other than the course designer and developer.)

Classical Approach

In a training program designed according to the classical approach—whose roots are in the lessons of ancient Greece—the instructor broadcasts content to learners through a lecture (live events and some self-study online tutorials) or extended essay (other self-study programs). Some learning professionals refer to this approach as the "sage on the stage" because it typifies the tradition of an expert transmitting knowledge to learners. Some also deride the approach as ineffective, but research reported by Winfred Arthur, Jr., Winston Bennett, Pamela Edens, and Suzanne Bell (2003) concludes that lectures can be just as effective as other instructional approaches.

Occasionally, the instructor will lecture without interruption. But a more effective application of the classical approach is when the instructor uses the lecture as the primary means of transmitting instructional material and complements the presentation with other learning activities. These might include screenings of videos and films, presentations by guest speakers, and classroom discussions resulting from questions posed by both the instructor and the learners.

The classical approach works best for content that must be transmitted as is, such as policies. For example, the content for the example course on how to apply the new security policy mentioned in earlier chapters might work well with the classical approach because learners must apply the content as is. The purpose of teaching is ensuring compliance with the policies, rather than just raising awareness of the issues.

 Think About This

Typically, a training program designed according to the classical approach follows this seven-step structure:
1. Gain learners' attention.
2. Present an overview of the content, including the learning objectives covered in the training program.
3. Present the learning material through a lecture or with the assistance of a video or similar audiovisual program.
4. Discuss the learning material.
5. Provide practice problems (either in class or as homework between class sessions).
6. Summarize the content.
7. Test learners.

One of the many advantages of the classical approach is that, at its simplest, it requires few special resources such as equipment or special instruction. But you do need to focus on some particular areas where support is likely to be needed.

- For lectures in live training programs, provide instructors with lecture notes that not only identify the key points to address, but also provide an additional level of depth of content so that an instructor whose knowledge of a particular aspect of the topic can still effectively present the material.
- For the presentation of instructional material in a self-study program (the equivalent of lecture), write out the presentation of material, word for word. The presentation takes the form of a script for narrated self-study programs and a text, like an article or book, for other self-study programs.
- For discussions in live training programs, provide instructors with discussion questions, anticipate correct and incorrect responses from learners, and suggest feedback from the instructor.
- For guest speakers (who present during a live training program and either through a recording or a transcript in a self-study program), provide appropriate guidance. For guest speakers in live events, provide the guest with the exact time and location (physical or virtual) of the presentation, the length of time available to speak, and an outline of the material you would like the guest to cover. Similarly, for guest speakers participating in a recording or contributing a transcript, provide background on the anticipated length of the recording and the material you would like the guest to cover. Although some might believe that telling guest speakers what you would like them to cover interferes with their presentation, most presenters actually appreciate this guidance. It helps them target their comments and make the most effective use of their and the class's time.
- For videos and other audiovisual resources used in live training programs, provide learners with instructions for using the materials. Start by stating what learners should get from the resource and how the material integrates with the rest of the program. Then, indicate whether to present the entire video or audiovisual resource or, if using only part, the exact minute and second at which to start playing the recording and the exact minute and second when to stop playing it.
- For practice problems and tests, provide answer keys and points to discuss when reviewing answers (such as insights into why people might have made common errors).

Because it is the most efficient to develop—requiring the least design and development time of all instructional strategies—the classical approach also works best when course designers and developers are pressed for time to develop a training program.

But beware. The classical approach also serves as the default strategy for most instructors because it is the instructional strategy with which they are familiar. Many designers use it not because it best meets the needs, but because it's the only strategy they know.

Mastery Learning

Mastery learning emerges from behavioral psychology, from which emerged the observation that mastering a significant skill (one named in the main objective) builds on the mastery of many smaller skills or tasks (supporting and subsupporting objectives). Educational psychologist Robert Gagne documented the approach in his 1985 book, *The Conditions of Learning and Theory of Instruction.*

A training program designed for mastery begins by gaining learners' attention. Then the instructor describes and demonstrates a skill learners must master. Learners practice the skill and continue doing so until they master it. The training program closes with a test or similar assessment to verify that learners have, indeed, mastered the skill.

One of the advantages of mastery learning is its straightforward approach to teaching: gain attention, teach, demonstrate, practice, and then test. Mastery learning is popular for teaching technical skills to novices, especially when learners must perform the skills in a prescribed manner. For example, trainers use mastery learning to teach software skills, manufacturing processes, basic customer service skills, performance management, and basic sales skills.

Instructors need extensive support

 Think About This

While mastery instruction is ideal for teaching novices—because it carefully sequences the instruction and verifies that learners have successfully mastered one objective before moving to the next—the pace often frustrates more experienced learners. In such instances, training programs merely instruct learners on variations of skills they already perform successfully and often repeat knowledge they have already mastered. Course designers and developers should adjust the structure to reflect the mastery of experienced learners, removing parts that would feel repetitive to them.

from course designers and developers to ensure effective mastery learning, especially during the demonstration and practice phases of instruction. Instructors need enough exercises (as many as 5–10 for each concept taught) to provide sufficient practice opportunities for learners who have difficulty mastering material. When preparing practice activities for live training programs, instructors need clear instructions for administering the activities and hints they can use to guide learners who get stuck. Instructors also need correct responses to activities, an explanation of why one particular response is correct, and anticipated incorrect responses and feedback to provide to learners about why their responses are not correct. Instructors use this information to determine what learners misunderstood and how they can correct that misunderstanding. Address the same issues when designing self-study programs, but note that the material is communicated directly to learners, rather than indirectly through an instructor as during live programs.

 Think About This

Typically, a training program designed according to the mastery learning model follows a nine-step structure (adapted from Gagne 1985):
1. Gain learners' attention.
2. Present an overview of the content, including the learning objectives covered in the training program.
3. Recall previous knowledge, so that learners can link new material to material they already know.
4. Explain the material.
5. Demonstrate the skill.
6. Let learners practice the skill under close supervision, receiving positive or negative feedback at each juncture.
7. Allow learners to continue practicing the skill, reducing the amount of feedback until they can perform the skill without assistance. For example, learners might only receive feedback if they make an incorrect choice.
8. Summarize the content.
9. Test or similarly assess learners.

Discovery Learning

For a training program designed for discovery learning, learners first encounter a problem that places them in a real-world experience. By responding to the problem, learners "discover" key learning points. A debriefing that follows elicits and reinforces these learning points. The initial problem can take many forms, such as a simulation or case study. Because discovery learning allows learners to discover concepts by experiencing them, some people refer to it as a type of experiential learning.

Discovery learning is useful for teaching skills in which learners must make judgments. For example, discovery learning is popular for teaching management decision making. It is also useful for teaching advanced troubleshooting skills, especially for people who service complex high-tech products in ways that go beyond existing documentation.

The heart of discovery learning is the activities. But learners often follow paths in these activities that differ from the anticipated ones. Therefore, one of the challenges in designing a training program following the discovery learning strategy is developing the activities. At the heart of the activities is the debriefings. Debriefings are mandatory to learning because learners often do not always discover key lessons on their own or incorrectly grasp them.

So when planning the debriefing, carefully plan it. To ensure that learners successfully master the underlying objectives, the debriefing must do more than merely identify the correct response, it also needs to explain why that response is correct and why other responses are not, so that learners can build the thought processes—or cognitive skills—the activity hopes to build. Furthermore, most responses have elements of correctness and incorrectness, and the distinction among the two might be too subtle for learners to recognize without assistance.

To provide that assistance, structure the debriefing like this (which works equally well in live and self-study training programs):

1. After preparing a correct response and anticipating several incorrect ones, begin the debriefing with a discussion of the least likely incorrect response. When discussing it, explain why learners might think this response is correct and then explain what makes this response less appropriate.

2. Do this for each of the other incorrect responses, ending with the response that is closest to the correct response.

3. Present the correct response. Start the discussion of it by explaining why learners might have overlooked it and then explain why it is the best solution in this situation.

Such a debriefing not only provides feedback on each possible response but also the thought processes underlying these responses.

Because course designers and developers must account for different learning approaches, discovery learning programs are more complex to design and develop—and thus may be more costly. This is especially true with online self-study programs, because the different responses must be built into the program.

Think About This

A discovery learning experience typically follows this format:

1. A brief introduction, which presents the main learning objective covered by the training program.
2. A problem for learners to address, which can take many different forms. The key challenge in choosing a problem for a unit using discovery learning is choosing one that richly represents the material to be addressed in the unit, yet remains simple enough that a novice can address it. Note, too, that the problem should be a learning experience, not a trick question. Among the possibilities you can consider are these:

   - a case study, which presents a richly described problem based on something that actually occurred, as well as the key issues underlying the problem, and asks learners to identify issues that a solution must address

   - a scenario, which presents a summarized version of a case (rather than a whole case), and asks learners to identify either the issues that must be addressed by the solution or whether the way that someone addressed the scenario was appropriate

   - a simulation, which presents the key components of an environment and allows learners to interact with the environment and experience the benefits of good choices and the consequences of poor ones.

3. Debriefing of the problem, which is typically an interactive discussion of tangible lessons from the experience. This discussion is followed by an exploration of learners' feelings about the activity. The discussion concludes by abstracting key learning points from the exercise.
4. Reinforcing the learning points by presenting them in more detail, with some additional supporting material.
5. Presenting a second learning problem (if needed) to give learners an opportunity to practice the skills.
6. Summarizing the key learning points.
7. Testing or similarly assessing the learners.

When designing a discovery lesson, spend as much time on the debriefing as learners need; this debriefing and the ensuing discussion are central to learning. Researchers Paul Kirschner, John Sweller, and Richard Clark (2006) have noted that minimal guidance—that is, little or no debriefing—does not work. Without the feedback, discovery learning often fails to achieve its objectives.

Performance Without Training

Sometimes, learners can achieve the intended objectives of a formal training program without going through it. For example, rather than teaching learners how to calculate a complicated commission formula, learners might be able to calculate commission if you provide them with a coded spreadsheet. The spreadsheet can prompt learners to enter information about sales and—

based on the product, special incentives in place, and agreements with the sales representative stored on the system—the spreadsheet would automatically calculate the commission.

Other learners might benefit from reminders of the skills learned in training that help them apply the skills in the workplace. For example, a programmer might have learned a number of commands in a training class, but he needs a quick reference to remember how to specifically use each.

These resources are called *job aids.* Providing job aids that help learners perform their work is one of the options for presenting material to learners. In some cases, you provide job aids to supplement a training program, providing learners with materials to help them easily apply concepts taught in class when they return to the job. In fact, many experienced course designers and developers include job aids with their programs to help learners transfer skills.

In other cases, you provide these resources in place of training programs if you have a high degree of confidence that workers will easily find the job aid and use it when needed. Providing job aids in place of training programs gives this approach its name: performance without training.

Job aids have become nearly ubiquitous. You've probably seen pocket-size laminated cards that serve as quick references and that workers can carry around. Similarly, cash registers in fast-food restaurants have pictures of items on the menu so cashiers do not need to remember prices. In offices, workers often create their own job aids, like the sticky notes with shortcuts jotted on them. Because job aids stand on their own, you must design them so learners can use them correctly without any training or outside assistance.

Choosing an Instructional Strategy

Choosing an instructional strategy is part science, part art, and part intuition. In some instances, you choose a single strategy for the entire training program. You might do so because the program is brief and only requires one strategy. Or you might do so because all the material is similar in nature and, by choosing the same strategy for teaching each part, you reinforce the relationships among the different units.

In other instances, the material in each unit is sufficiently different that the training program benefits from different strategies for each unit. Or you might choose different approaches in each unit to provide variety for the learners.

Choose a strategy that works for the instructional material (some instructional material lends itself to particular instructional strategies), the learning environment (some strategies might require resources that are not available), and your preferences (some strategies make you feel most comfortable). A good learning strategy reflects a balance among these three needs.

You might need to alter your plans if the practical realities of the training situation hinder your ability to effectively use a strategy. For example, suppose that a course designer wanted to use mastery learning to teach learners to print the word *Confidential* in the running header of each page of a workbook. Later, the course designer finds out that the classroom where the training program will be taught does not have computers for learners to use and is not likely to get them. The course designer must change the instructional strategy to match the practical realities of the classroom. Rather than mastery learning, the course designer might instead choose to demonstrate this skill as a part of the lecture (classical model).

In the end, the strategy that you choose is the one that you feel will work most effectively in a given learning context and that you feel most comfortable using. But some course designers and developers only feel comfortable with just one or two instructional strategies, and their training programs start to seem monotonous. The more strategies that course designers and developers can integrate into their designs, the more varied—and thus engaging—the learning experiences they can offer.

Presenting Design Plans

To inform stakeholders about how you plan to present the course material and gain their support for your approach, formally document the design plans. Although each organization handles the presentation of design plans in its own way, design plans are, generally, brief documents that present the following:

- brief background on the project (approximately 100 words), including who requested it, the purpose of the program (especially the desired end result), intended learners, and the anticipated business benefit. This repeats information about the analysis and requirements presented to stakeholders (see chapter 4) and provides a context for stakeholders, most of whose primary interests differ from this program and won't remember these details
- information map, showing the general structure of the program
- brief (one paragraph) description of the format, medium, and overall instructional strategy (along with an explanation of the choices if they differ from the request)

- brief descriptions of each major unit, with a one-sentence description of the purpose of the unit, a list of the main and supporting objectives covered, a one- to two-sentence description of the instructional strategy, and an outline for the unit that indicates the sequence of major events in the unit and a general description of the nature of activities (do not provide in-depth details).

In some situations, especially when the course designer and developer works for a different employer than the one sponsoring the training program, the course designer and developer shares the plans in a brief (15-minute) formal presentation before providing the written plans.

Stakeholders will provide feedback on the plans. Typical issues that arise during the review pertain to the technical content (usually issues of clarity and accuracy), clarifications of the instructional strategy, and information about related programs with which this one shares similarities. As a result of those similarities, stakeholders might suggest that you adjust the plans to strengthen the consistency with the related material or reuse that material in this program. After revising the plans to reflect the comments from stakeholders, request that the sponsor or a representative officially approve the plan, providing you the support needed to proceed with the more costly development of the program.

Platinum, Silver, and Bronze Types of Projects

Like the processes described in previous chapters, the selection process described in this chapter pertains to a platinum, or top-of-the-line, training project. The process of selecting an instructional strategy for silver and bronze projects does not differ from the description here. However, the realities of the situation usually outweigh the needs of the instructional material and your preferences when choosing a strategy for silver and bronze projects. Budgets are more constrained for these projects because of their more-limited scope and visibility. Similarly, the schedules for these projects are often more constrained because sponsors request the projects just before they need the program. As a result, course designers and developers often lack the resources needed to design discovery learning programs, especially ones involving simulation. Designers might consider slightly scaled back discovery learning activities for silver and bronze projects (such as a case study rather than a simulation).

Similarly, when designing revisions to existing programs, course designers and developers need to consider the instructional strategies used in the existing materials. When the changes affect material within an existing lesson, course designers and developers should retain the existing strategy to minimize unnecessary revisions. When adding new sections, they must seamlessly integrate with existing sections that are not revised. Use similar strategies with new material that were used in the existing parts; jarring changes in instructional strategy from one section to the next could confuse learners.

Getting It Done

Choosing an instructional strategy for presenting the instructional content starts with some general considerations for creating a motivating, active, and supportive learning environment. Next comes selecting an overall strategy for presenting the material and specific strategies for individual units; these strategies include the classical approach, mastery learning, discovery learning, and performance without training. The decision of which strategy to use balances three competing needs: the needs of the instructional material, practicalities of the situation, and your preferences. At the end of this process, document the design plans and formally present them to stakeholders to receive their approval and permission to proceed.

Use Exercise 6-1 to guide you through the choice of an instructional strategy and for presenting the design plans for a project on which you are working.

Exercise 6-1. Presenting the Design Plans

A brief background on the project—requester, purpose (especially intended end result), learners, business benefit—based on material included in the analysis and requirements. Limit to 100 words.
Information map of the program (prepared in chapter 5)
Brief (one paragraph) description of the format, medium, and overall instructional strategy (along with an explanation of the choice if it differs from the request)
Brief descriptions of unit 1: • one-sentence description of the purpose of the unit • list the main and supporting objectives covered • one- to two-sentence description of the instructional strategy • outline for the unit that indicates the sequence of major events in the unit and a general description of the nature of activities (do not provide in-depth details) **[Repeat for each unit in the program]**

7

The Basics of Developing Instructional Materials

 What's Inside This Chapter

This chapter starts a three-chapter sequence that explains how to develop the materials used in training programs. Specifically, this chapter identifies the materials you need to develop and explains how to prepare:

- Materials for live training programs
- Materials for self-study training programs
- Common parts of training programs, including openings, instructions for interactive activities, and closings.

An exercise at the end of this chapter helps you choose the materials needed for live and self-study training programs.

Getting Started With Development

The last two chapters explored the process of design—of thinking through the plan for presenting the instructional material so that it achieves the objectives for the training program. Design decisions included choosing the format (live or self-study) and communication medium (face-to-face, online, or print) used to deliver the material to learners, structuring the program and units (including front and back matter), and choosing the instructional strategy—the approach to presenting and developing skills. These decisions force designers to consider their approach to the training program and make sure that they can develop the program within the time and budget available. This reduces cost in the long run, because you reduce the likelihood of developing materials that you might have to scrap later. After completing the design plans, you present them to stakeholders for review and approval.

With approved design plans, you can start developing program materials that follow the plans: prepare the materials described in the plans and ready them for distribution to others. This chapter begins a three-chapter sequence that describes the development process. This chapter describes the materials included in live and self-study training programs and how to prepare the common parts of training programs, including openings, instructions for interactive activities, and closings.

Chapter 8 describes some of the key tasks involved in developing programs, including writing text, designing visuals, and producing materials. Chapter 9 concludes the discussion of development by describing the processes used to ensure that the training program is clear and accurate and operates without problems before it is made available to learners.

Preparing Materials for Live Training Programs

When preparing a live training program, you prepare two general categories of materials: a student guide and the instructor guide. The student guide usually consists of a copy of all the slides used in the program (called *visuals*), activities, and supplemental information (such as relevant articles, fact sheets, and job aids). The instructor guide includes an annotated copy of the visuals in the program, suggesting what the instructor should say during a lecture. It also contains an annotated version of the activities, including instructions for setting up the activities, helping learners during them, and conducting the debriefing, in addition to a copy of the materials provided to learners.

Preparing the Student Guide

The student guide provides learners with the materials they need to complete the training program: visuals, activities, and supplemental information.

Basic Rule 24

A student guide is a self-contained package that learners use both in class and as a reference on the job. It contains a copy of the visuals (usually slides), which provides a record of the conversation in the classroom and that most students use to take notes during class. A student guide also contains materials needed to complete the activities and supplemental information that learners might use to prepare for the program, during activities, and on the job.

Visuals

The backbone of nearly every training program is the visuals, which usually take the form of slides. For learners, visuals provide a record of key words or points to follow during class. Visuals help learners reconnect with the conversation if their attention lapses (a likely situation because learners can listen three or four times faster than an instructor can speak). Visuals also illustrate concepts. For example, in a course on security policies, a picture of a page marked *Confidential* on a slide shows learners exactly how to identify confidential material in printed documents. Although not a transcript of the training program, visuals represent the closest thing to one, so learners like to have copies of them as a reference when they return to their jobs.

Each visual should present one distinct idea using a limited number of words, ideally no more than 25–30. The assertion-evidence approach to designing visuals provides a framework for producing clear, compelling slides that effectively communicate a single idea in a limited number of words. The approach, based on ideas in Nancy Duarte's 2008 book *slide:ology*, suggests that each slide make an assertion and have evidence to illuminate the assertion.

Basic Rule 25

Visuals serve as a reminder, not a script, so limit amount of material placed on them.

The assertion is a brief sentence (20–25 words) that provokes thought and discussion (Price 2013). It appears at the top of the visual in the area reserved for a heading. The evidence can take four forms: 1) illustrations, which show processes and concepts; 2) charts, which show relationships between numbers; 3) symbols, which represent abstract concepts; and 4) additional points in a bulleted list.

Figure 7-1 shows a generic template for creating a visual following the assertion-evidence approach. Figure 7-2 shows a sample slide.

Figure 7-1. Generic Template for Creating a Visual Following the Assertion-Evidence Approach

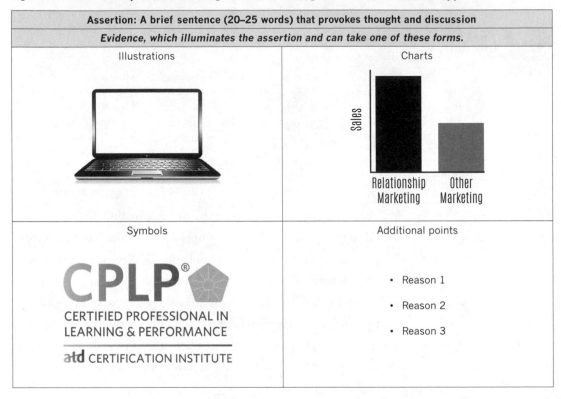

Until someone actually presents them in a classroom, no one knows exactly how many visuals an instructor will have time to go through in a class session. However, you can use past experience and the experience of other instructors to estimate an appropriate number of slides for a training program. Table 7-1 suggests some general guidelines.

Figure 7-2. Generic Template for Creating a Visual Following the Assertion-Evidence Approach

Table 7-1. Determining the Number of Visuals to Use

Program Length	Program Speed	Estimated Total Number of Visuals
Fewer than eight minutes	One visual per minute	Eight or fewer
Eight to 30 minutes	Approximately one visual for every three minutes	Four to 10
30 to 90 minutes	Approximately one visual for every three to five minutes	Six to 30
More than 90 minutes	Approximately one visual for every eight to 10 minutes (this includes time for class discussions and activities, which often do not involve visuals)	10 or more

Most course designers and developers use presentation graphics software to create, display, and publish visuals, such as Microsoft PowerPoint or Apple Keynote. Regardless of the program used, all provide the same general capabilities for creating, displaying, and publishing visuals. The capabilities with which you should become familiar include:

- Templates, which let you start a new presentation quickly. Templates typically include preset slides with typefaces, colors, and other design features and reflect the organization's brand.
- Outline view, which lets you quickly start creating the specific visuals for your program. By starting in outline view, you can quickly insert front and back matter and, for the rest of the slides, write the assertion statements for each visual and note the points to include for the evidence. You can use outline view even when starting with an existing template.

- Tables, charts, and artwork, which let you easily create visual components within the presentation graphics application to include in the evidence section of the slides.
- Headers and footers, which let you easily insert slide numbers. These numbers provide a signpost to help learners follow the program.
- Printing, which lets you print a set of visuals in various formats, to provide handouts for learners.

Activities

To complete learning activities, learners need the necessary materials and information. First, they need the purpose of the activity.

In addition, for case studies and similar activities, learners next need instructions for preparing the case for class, as well as background information about the case, questions to respond to, forms to complete, or similar types of materials.

For computer-based activities, learners need step-by-step instructions for completing the activity, as well as usernames and passwords to gain access to the equipment or software, hints for working past known trouble spots, and illustrations showing what correct and incorrect solutions look like and what caused them.

Figure 7-3 shows an example of an activity for a management training course.

Figure 7-3. Activity for a Management Training Course

Activity 1: Hiring Discussion

Instructions
1. Read the following scenarios.
2. Indicate whether the manager handled the situation appropriately or inappropriately.
(And, as the business world requires that managers make decisions, you, too, must choose one of the alternatives listed.)

What the Manager Did:	These Actions Were (Choose One, No Fair Saying "I Don't Know"):	
Bill manages one of five technical communication departments at the development lab for a major software manufacturer. Bill's lab is in a smaller community (about 50,000 people), two hours from the nearest major metropolitan area. While speaking to a class of seniors in the technical communication program at a major university in a major metropolitan area, Bill responded as follows to a student question about XML: "Well, if you don't know it, we wouldn't even consider hiring you."	❑ Appropriate	❑ Inappropriate
Phyllis manages a documentation department of 10 women, mostly over age 40, and two men. She recently gave a second interview to Rich, a brash 24-year-old. He's very qualified for the job and Jessica, the lead writer he would work most closely with, seems to think he'd work well. But Phyllis found Rich to be a bit pushy in the interview and decides not to hire him, because she's afraid she'd be managing too much "broken glass."	❑ Appropriate	❑ Inappropriate

Reprinted with permission from Saul Carliner. 1998–2015. All rights reserved.

Supplemental Material

Supplemental material provides learners with information and resources that they might find useful back on the job. In some instances, learners also use this material in class.

Although the exact nature of supplemental materials varies among programs, Table 7-2 suggests materials that learners might find helpful for particular types of programs.

Table 7-2. Supplemental Material to Provide Learners

For This Type of Training	Provide This Supplemental Information
Product training	• Product information, such as brochures and fact sheets • Testimonials from customers who participated in pilots • Technical articles by product engineers and programmers (after receiving permission to publish any copyrighted material) • Reference material that might be needed to complete activities in class and address situations in the field, such as quick reference sheets that list codes widely used in the job
Marketing training	• Articles about sales techniques and the product line from marketing magazines (after receiving permission to republish any copyrighted material) • Quick reference material about products • Instructions for placing orders, especially if doing so is even moderately complex
Management development	• Copies of corporate policies (as well as links so learners can find the most current versions of the policies) • Copies of forms (when needed), as well as links to the forms • Articles about management issues from corporate newsletters, magazines, and popular press (after receiving permission to republish any copyrighted material)
Pharmaceutical training	• Product information, such as brochures and fact sheets • Testimonials from customers who participated in trials • Technical articles by medical staff and product scientists (after receiving permission to republish any copyrighted material) • Other relevant articles from the scientific and trade press (request permission to reprint these, too) • Other scientific reference material relevant to the product
New employee orientation	• Copy of the employee handbook (if your organization has one) • Information about employee benefits (if not already distributed to them), as well as a link to the site with more complete information • Information about the company's products, services, and history
Manufacturing training	• Reference material that staff needs while performing manufacturing processes • Information about the product that staff is assembling
Safety training	Signs, warnings, and similar job aids to post in the work place to remind learners about safety on the job

Assembling the Student Guide

After preparing the visuals, activities, and supplemental materials, assemble them into a single student guide. Usually you assemble these materials using a word processor or desktop publishing program. A typical student guide follows this structure:

1. title page

2. edition notice (page with copyright statements)

3. table of contents

4. visuals

5. activities

6. supplemental information

7. references and other sources of information

8. evaluation form.

Some or all of the front and back matter might come from an existing template.

Note that the student guides for face-to-face and virtual classes are the same. The primary issue is distribution. For face-to-face classes, many organizations still print copies of the student guide and distribute it in the classroom. But many other organizations electronically distribute it for face-to-face classes before the class. For virtual classes, nearly all organizations electronically distribute the student guide before the class. Most organizations prefer distributing the electronic materials in a Portable Document Format (PDF), because that format ensures that the materials students receive are formatted as the course designer and developer intended. Some organizations send the materials by email before the class, and others through a learning management system, which learners sign in to and download the materials.

Preparing the Instructor Guide

The instructor guide provides materials needed to administer the training program and lead class sessions. The instructor guide is typically an annotated version of the student guide. Specifically, an instructor guide contains setup instructions, annotated visuals to use in lectures, instructions for administering learning activities, and a close-out list for completing the program.

Setup Instructions

Setup instructions serve as a to-do list for preparing and running a class session. For face-to-face classes, instructions include how to set up and operate audiovisual equipment and arrange the classroom furniture. For virtual classes, they explain how to upload slides, set up interactive questions and polls, and establish groups (if needed). For all types of classes, identify materials needed for demonstrations and learning activities, software and files used in the training program, and other materials needed.

Basic Rule 26

When writing the instructor guide, assume that someone else will serve as the instructor for the training program. Even if you might teach the program yourself, write the instructor guide for another instructor anyway. If for any reason you are not available to teach, another instructor can easily fill in.

Annotated Visuals for Lectures

The annotated visuals include notes that guide the instructor through the discussion associated with that slide. Figure 7-4 shows an example of an annotated visual from a management training program.

Most course designers and developers provide notes for each image or bullet point on a visual, list anticipated questions from learners, and suggest responses to those anticipated questions. The notes should also provide slightly more in-depth material than intended for learners, so instructors can handle unanticipated questions. Using the notes alone, instructors should have enough information to communicate the intended message and comfortably address questions even in those rare situations in which the instructor has limited subject matter expertise.

When writing notes, avoid a word-for-word script. Instructors are not likely to memorize it. Or worse, they will read it word for word, which will bore learners. Scripting prevents instructors from illuminating the material with their own experiences, something that engages learners and builds credibility for the instructor.

 Noted

Most presentation graphics software such as Microsoft PowerPoint lets you annotate the slides as you create them. You do so using the "Notes" view of the slide. The screen has a section where you type the notes. The software also provides options for printing the notes with the slides.

Figure 7-4. Annotated Slide

Review Incentives

- **Salary and benefits**
- **Signing bonuses**
- **Additional vacation**
- **Training**

NOTES

Review Incentives: The entire offer package matters, not just the bottom-line salary.

Salary and benefits: Salary might be competitive but also need to see how benefits stack up. Medical co-pays? Flex time? Family leave?

Signing bonuses: Have been popular. Way of making up for a lower salary without raising base salary.

Additional vacation: Especially useful for experienced workers, who are concerned about losing accrued vacation time by jumping to another company.

Training: Studies suggest that the ability to develop new skills attracts new workers. One way of demonstrating this commitment is the amount of training promised.

Anticipated questions:

My company is not willing to review these. What can I do?

Response: Document cases when your first-choice candidate specifically rejected your offer because of one of these issues and build a case for HR to review organizational policies.

Instructions for Administering Learning Activities

Instructors usually need significantly more information about learning activities than learners do. For example, to start an activity, instructors need instructions on how to prepare for it and introduce it to learners. Consider these instructions for starting a case study activity:

> "First, point out the page number of the activity in the student guide. Second, divide learners into teams of approximately five people. Then, give learners about 15 minutes to discuss the case."

When running the activity, instructors need information on how to resolve anticipated problems that might arise, a complete description of the solution and how to reach it, and a list of anticipated wrong responses—and how to fix them.

When concluding the activity, instructors need a guide for running the debriefing discussion, because the real learning usually occurs during this conversation. Figure 7-5 shows an example of the instructor guide for debriefing the first scenario presented in Figure 7-3.

Figure 7-5. A Guide for a Post-Activity Discussion for the First Scenario in Figure 7-3

Debriefing Bill

Case: Bill manages one of five technical communication departments at the development lab for a major software manufacturer. Bill's lab is in a smaller community (about 50,000 people), two hours from the nearest major metropolitan area. While speaking to a class of seniors in the technical communication program at a major university in a major metropolitan area, Bill responded as follows to a student question about XML: "Well, if you don't know it, we wouldn't even consider hiring you."

1. Ask people to raise their hands if they thought Bill's actions were appropriate. Then ask people to raise their hands if they thought Bill's actions were inappropriate.
2. Ask people who thought the actions were appropriate to explain why.
3. Anticipated responses: These are the skills we need on the job. One needs to be clear about expectations, starting with the hiring process.
4. Ask people who thought the actions were inappropriate to explain why.
5. Anticipated responses: These skills are secondary to the job. The primary skills are communication abilities. Bill's statement will scare off good candidates who don't have these secondary skills, which can be learned on the job. Recruiting young people in large metropolitan areas to take jobs in smaller communities is a challenge.

Learning Points

- Admit that learners do not have the entire picture. Tight competition exists for the students graduating from this program.
- Note that the real skill that Bill wants is communication skills; XML is a tool needed to complete the job.
- The approach was popular when skilled labor was more plentiful.
- By hiring for software skills over the more central communication skills needed to complete the job, Bill might be discounting otherwise qualified candidates.
- Before going into the hiring process, review the job qualifications to make sure that the job description you write attracts the kinds of candidates who will really meet your needs (the objective of the unit).

The way that you administer learning activities varies, depending on the type of activity. Table 7-3 provides some guidance on the materials needed for four common instructional activities: general discussions, case studies, computer-based activities, and instructional games.

Table 7-3. Materials Needed to Administer Various Types of Learning Activities

Learning Activity	Introducing the Activity	Running the Activity	Managing the Postactivity Debriefing
General discussions	Explain how the learning activity relates to the objectives.	• Provide discussion questions. • Anticipate responses from students, and include them in the instructor guides. • Suggest replies to the anticipated responses.	Label and reinforce the learning points. With these points identified, they can be presented in more detail with additional support. For example, if the discussion explored approaches to handling a discipline problem in the workplace, this part of the debriefing might present the most common strategies for addressing behavior problems and corporate policies regarding persistent behavior problems. This information might also be part of the visuals.
Computer-based activities	• Describe its purpose. In addition to explaining the overall purpose of the activity, also explain how the activity fits into the goal of the course, and the objectives of the unit in which it is included. • Provide instructions for performing the activity. • Demonstrate the activity, if needed. • Divide learners into groups, if needed.	• Provide a copy of the instructions given to learners. • For each step in the instructions given to learners, provide the instructor with a list of anticipated problems and suggest how to coach learners past them. • Provide sample files if learners need to use material that is already stored in the computer. • Arrange for accounts and passwords for students to use so that learners can access content on the computer.	• Review the results, and provide a visual example of a successfully completed project. • Ask learners what they did—where they went right and where they went wrong. • Offer suggestions for performing the task in a work setting.

(continued)

131

Table 7-3. Materials Needed to Administer Various Types of Learning Activities (continued)

Learning Activity	Introducing the Activity	Running the Activity	Managing the Postactivity Debriefing

Case studies	• Explain how the learning activity relates to the objectives.
	• Point out the location of guiding questions that learners should answer when preparing the case (if any).
	• State the form of the response (if a particular format is required).
		Give copy of the case study to learners.	• Discuss possible solutions. Usually these cases have no clear-cut right and wrong answers, but ones that are more or less appropriate.
			  ○ Start with the least appropriate solution. First explain why learners might have chosen it, and then explain why it is not correct.
			  ○ Continue the discussion of the rest of the less appropriate solutions, in reverse order, using the same structure as for the first incorrect solution.
			  ○ End with a discussion of the most appropriate solution. Start by explaining why learners might not have chosen it, and then explain why it is the most appropriate.
			• Provide a discussion guide for the debriefing that addresses the following points in this order:
			  ○ Discuss tangible experiences from the experience.
			  ○ Explore learners' feelings about the activity and the learning experience.
			  ○ Identify the key learning points from the activity.
			  ○ Label and reinforce these learning points. With the points identified, they can be presented in more detail. For example, the case might have explored business strategy. This part of the debriefing might name three principles to consider when planning a business strategy. The discussion points might also be part of the visuals.

Table 7-3. Materials Needed to Administer Various Types of Learning Activities (continued)

Learning Activity	Introducing the Activity	Running the Activity	Managing the Postactivity Debriefing
Instructional games	• Explain how the learning activity relates to the objectives. • Provide instructions for performing the game. • If needed, divide participants into groups to play the game.	• Provide annotated instructions given to learners. The notes should identify known problem areas and offer suggestions that the instructor can give to learners for working past the problems. • Provide game materials as needed such as a board, cards, dice, and playing pieces for physical games or user IDs and passwords for computer-based games.	• Discuss tangible lessons from the experience. • Explore learners' feelings about the activity and the learning experience. • Identify the key learning points from the activity. • Label and reinforce the learning points, as you would do when debriefing a case study.

Close-Out List

The tasks that the instructor must complete after the class ends include grading tests (if any), returning materials, and conducting follow-up communications with learners. Close-out activities vary depending on the characteristics of the training program and its learners, and ongoing habits within the organization sponsoring the program.

Assembling the Instructor Guide

After preparing the instructor's notes, instructions for administering the learning activities, and close-out list, assemble these pieces into a single instructor guide. Usually you do so through your word processor or desktop publishing program. A typical instructor's guide follows this structure:

1. title page (same as for student guide, but with the words *Instructor's Guide* on the cover)

2. edition notice (page with copyright statements)

3. table of contents (most word processors will automatically produce this; see the next chapter for information on how)

4. setup instructions

5. visuals with instructor's notes on the page

6. instructor's version of the learning activities (including the guide to leading the debriefing)

7. supplemental materials

8. close-out list.

Most organizations store a digital version of the instructor's guide in a place where instructors can easily find it. Instructors print the guide before starting a class.

Preparing Materials for Self-Study Training Programs

Self-study programs take two general forms: an online tutorial or a workbook. Online tutorials, in turn, have three levels of complexity. (Also called Levels 1, 2, and 3 like the levels in the Kirkpatrick evaluation framework described in chapters 1 and 4, do not confuse the overlapping terminology and their meanings, as they are distinct.)

Level 1 e-learning, the least complex and most common, includes a recording of a slide presentation (usually called a *slidecast*) as well as some outside readings, simple activities (such as multiple-choice questions), and assignments performed outside of the tutorial (such as essays).

Level 2 e-learning includes either a slidecast or slides that learners read on their own, often interspersed with videos of scenes of work processes, animations, outside readings, and simple to complex activities, such as multiple-choice questions, drag-and-drop activities, and simple simulations of software applications.

Basic Rule 27

Include all the material needed to complete the course in a self-study training program because learners have no other source of instruction or guidance.

Level 3 e-learning, the most complex and least common, usually includes significant original and staged video (such as videotaped scenes), custom animations, and simulated versions of business operations, customer exchanges, and management challenges.

In contrast with tutorials, workbooks are usually self-contained and provide all the materials a learner needs to complete a program; some may direct learners to activities—and tell them when to return to the workbook and continue the lesson.

Whether an online tutorial or a workbook, a self-study program contains several types of materials:

- A lecture, which usually takes the form of either a recording of an instructor narrating slides (levels 1 and 2 e-learning), a video (levels 2 and 3 e-learning), materials to read (levels 1, 2, and 3 e-learning and workbooks), and annotated slides similar to the ones you would include in an instructor's guide for a live training program but written in complete sentences or a book-like narrative (workbooks).
- Activities similar to the ones used in a live training program, but designed for learners to perform individually, on their own, at their own pace.
- Solutions to these activities, with the same level of detail provided in an instructor's guide for a live training program but written in full and polished sentences to be read by learners.
- Supplemental materials, the same types of readings, references, and related resources provided with live training programs.

Preparing a self-study-based training program is similar to preparing a live program, with a few adjustments. Table 7-4 suggests the structure of a self-study program, and how preparing these materials differs from preparing them for a live training program.

Table 7-4. Structure of a Self-Study Course

Item	How to Prepare
Title page, slide, or screen	Same as you would do for a live program.
Edition notice	For an online tutorial, usually present at the bottom of the title screen or slide, or in a section called *About*. For a workbook, handle it the same as you would for a student guide for a live program.
Table of contents	For an online tutorial, present a menu of units, usually immediately after the title screen. Buttons placed on the side or top of the screen usually help learners display the menu whenever they want. Most e-learning authoring tools automatically provide these links for you. For a workbook, handle the same as you would for a live program. For both types, use sequence numbers like Unit 1, Unit 2, and so forth, in the headings of units if you recommend that learners follow units in a particular order. Learners appreciate the explicit recommendation.
Introduction to the course	Provide a brief introduction to the program, unless you do so in the first unit. The introduction engages learners with the instructional material, presents the objectives, and highlights of the program.
Units	Present entire units as one whole that integrates lectures and activities, often going back and forth between the two. This is the same for online tutorials and workbooks. Typically, a unit includes front matter, instructional material activities, and back matter.
Summary	Close the program with a formal summary of material. Because it represents the last opportunity you have to reinforce the material, you might formally summarize the content even if you ask learners to do so also. See the discussion of summaries later in this chapter.
Test or similar assessment	Close the self-study program with an assessment of the extent to which learners mastered the objectives.
Supplemental material	For the most part, handle the same as you would provide for a live training program. But in an online self-study program, you can provide links to the materials, rather than having to duplicate them. This is especially useful for materials that frequently change, such as employee policies, price lists, and organizational news.
References and other resources	For the most part, handle the same as you would for a live training program. But in an online self-study program, you can provide links to the materials, rather than having to duplicate them.
Evaluation form	Provide instructions on how to submit the evaluation. For online programs, organizations typically conduct the evaluation online using survey software so provide a link to the software and any instructions learners might need to complete it. For workbooks, either provide a link to an online survey or, if learners complete a paper survey and return it, provide an addressed, postage-paid envelope to simplify this process.

When developing online self-study materials also consider these unique issues. First, prepare slides according to the assertion-evidence approach described earlier in this chapter, whether preparing them for slidecasts or screens for learners to read.

Second, for material that someone will narrate (such as slidecasts and videos), prepare a complete script. Doing so ensures that the narrator correctly records the instructional content. Many organizations hire narrators for their vocal talents, not their content expertise. State exactly what they should say; these narrators cannot improvise. Narrators who are not professional voice talents appreciate the explicit instructions on what to say.

 Think About This

When you prepare materials for online self-study programs, do not prepare slides and notes. Instead, prepare storyboards, which present all the material on a single screen or slide in the sequence of the online program along with any related instructions for producing it. In this way, others can review the planned screen or slide before costly production of the material starts. Some organizations use the term wireframes rather than storyboards. Storyboards include:

- A mock-up of the screen or slide with all the material that would appear on it in the location where it should appear. Note that graphics and illustrations are typically presented as stick drawings, words, or snapshots from a smartphone rather than finished artwork.
- Production instructions, which appear below the mock-up of the screen or slide (if prepared using Microsoft PowerPoint or Apple Keynote, place these in the Notes section), and include a word-for-word draft of the narration, instructions for sound effects, animation, producing visuals, and video shots (such as "fade in").
- Programming instructions, which appear below the production instructions (if presenting slides, place them in the Notes section, too) and tell programmers how to process all of the buttons on the screen as well as respond to any input that learners might enter. For example, if the system is supposed to display particular feedback when learners type "c" in response to a question, state "If learners enter 'c,' display this text."

See Figure 7-6 for an example of a storyboard.

For material that learners will read, write the material as if you were writing an article or book. Because learners do not have direct access to an instructor when reading the learning material, make sure that the material is clear enough for learners to understand without assistance.

Figure 7-6. Storyboard

Learning objective: When preparing or reviewing a resume, avoid the general resume don'ts.
Production instructions: When the screen opens, play narration: "Let's see what you already know about what not to include in your resume. Answer the question and find out!"
Programming instructions: (1) Make Exit, Back, Next, Play, Pause, and Stop buttons available as soon as the page is opened. (2) If learner clicks Play, run narration. (3) If learner clicks Pause, stop narration. (4) If learner clicks Stop, halt narration. (5) If learner clicks Back, go to previous page (screen 13: Section 2: What Should I Not Put in My Resume?). (6) If learner clicks Next, go to next page (screen 15: Common Resume Mistakes). (7) If learner clicks Exit, pop up a window asking "Are you sure you want to Exit?"; if learner clicks Yes, go to screen 5 (page: Structure of the Course), but if learner clicks No, close the pop-up window and stay on screen 14. (8) Add radio button next to each choice of answers. (True/False). (9) Only analyze the response after learner clicks Submit. (10) When learner clicks Submit, store answer in the Excel format in a record for this learner. (11) If learner chooses B (False), highlight the correct answer in green and place a green checkmark next to it. (12) If learner chooses A (True), place a red X mark next to it, and highlight the correct answer in green, but do not put a checkmark next to the correct answer.

Created by Andrada Muntean. Used with permission.

When developing activities for any type of self-study program, make sure that the instructions are as detailed as those provided to an instructor in a live program. As part of the activity materials, provide the solution. In online self-study programs, you can also provide feedback to responses from learners so include sample responses in the instructional materials. For complex activities, such as case studies and simulations of workplace activities, also provide the complete debriefing of the activity in the instructional materials. The level of detail provided should be similar to that provided in the instructor's guide for a live program, but written in polished sentences.

After developing the materials, you prepare them for distribution to learners. In nearly all cases, you distribute materials electronically. The information provided with the software used to produce the program explains how to produce materials that you can distribute to learners, such as PDF files of documents, and audio and video recordings in formats that learners can use on their devices.

Preparing Common Parts of Training Programs

Whether developing a live or self-study training program, the beginning, middle, and end pose unique challenges. The beginning provides the opportunity to introduce the instructional material and create a supportive learning environment. The middle introduces and demonstrates skills, and provides learners with opportunities to develop those skills. The ending provides an opportunity to remind learners of the key points they should recall and motivate them to apply the skills mastered in training and continue their learning of the subject.

Beginning of a Training Program

Like the first paragraph of a news article, the beginning of a training program must grab the learners' interest, summarize the points to follow, and relate the instructional material to learners' needs. In educational terms, the beginning of a program is called an *advance organizer.* Designed effectively, advance organizers can facilitate learning and retention, according to a review of several studies on advance organizers (Luiten, Ames, and Ackerson 1980).

For an effective beginning to a face-to-face training program, try jumping right into the program with a group activity, perhaps even before introducing the subject. This lets learners immerse themselves in the instructional material immediately while also providing an opportunity to network with other learners. This activity might serve as a fun way to review prerequisite skills or pique learners' curiosity about the program. For example, consider Figure 7-7, an activity to start a training program on security procedures mentioned earlier in this book. It presents the range of scenarios addressed by the program content while actively challenging learners to assess their presumed knowledge about the subject.

Use the debriefing of the activity to introduce the program and its main objectives or agenda. This preview of the content is the heart of the advance organizer because it signals the key content of the program to the learner.

Figure 7-7. An Activity for Starting a Program

Instructions
1. Introduce yourself to the other members of your group.
2. Working in groups, determine whether the employee acted appropriately in the following scenario. If you cannot reach consensus, indicate so.

    Scenario One: Michael, Jill, and Nicholas go to lunch in the employee cafeteria immediately after a heated meeting about their confidential new product. The point of contention in the meeting was the inclusion of three features in the product. The three of them debrief the meeting at lunch.

    The employees:

    ❑ Acted appropriately. Why? _____

    ❑ Did not act appropriately. Why? _____

    ❑ Our group cannot reach consensus. Why? _____

You can adapt an activity like this to start a live virtual class or a self-study program. Although learners would perform the activity on their own, starting immediately with an activity engages them by asking them to match wits with the instructor and, in the case of live virtual classes, fellow students. The primary difference would be in how you facilitate the responses, so make sure that the design takes into account the mediated communication.

 Noted

Some instructors start face-to-face training programs by asking learners to introduce themselves, and explain why they want to attend. Bad idea! Although introductions might seem like a great way to foster networking, think carefully about using them. These introductions often take too long (as long as 30 minutes in a large class, about 10 percent of the class time in a one-day program) and end up boring learners after the third or fourth introduction.

In contrast, because online learning can be anonymous, integrating networking into the program removes some of the unfamiliarity. But rather than use class time for such introductions, course designers and developers encourage learners to provide profiles that other participants in the program can view. Most learning management systems provide a means for learners to create a profile to share. Course designers and developers merely need to explicitly invite learners to create profiles before class and to view one another's profiles before or after class.

Middle of a Training Program

Although the design plans for a program provide a general structure for each unit, suggest the sequence in which to present material, and suggest the instructional strategy, staying on topic remains one of the most significant challenges for designers. While explaining content, the temptation is high to add an interesting—but slightly off-topic—real-world story that does not exactly relate to the material, or an ancillary fact that is interesting but does not directly further achievement of objectives.

When developing the middle, double-check to make sure that the content in those materials directly relates to the objectives. Lectures, activities, and materials associated with them that do not address one or more objectives distract learners from achieving the program's intended end result. So if you have a great case study to present but it does not directly relate to the objectives, choose another learning activity that will help learners achieve the objectives.

One way to keep activities on track is to lift them directly from the bank of test questions created during the analysis process. In this way, you ensure that they are relevant. Use the anticipated responses and resulting feedback you prepared when writing the testquestions as a starting point for the debriefings.

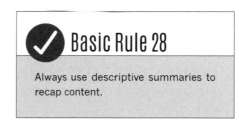

Basic Rule 28

Always use descriptive summaries to recap content.

Close each unit by summarizing the material. If possible, first ask learners to summarize the material in their own words. This informally assesses whether learners actually understood the content. Follow that with your own summary of the material. When doing so, you should use a descriptive summary.

Descriptive summaries repeat the main points of a unit or program so that learners can apply the material. Don't confuse them with topic summaries, which only name the topics but provide no details about them. Because the summary provides the last opportunity to remind learners of the key points, it should provide more detail than just the topics.

Consider this topic summary of the unit introducing the training program on relationship marketing:

> "This lesson introduced relationship marketing."

Note how the topic summary only mentions the key point of the presentation and does not tell learners what to remember. Learners who missed the earlier discussion must then review their materials to fully recall the main point, a great deal of work.

In contrast, consider this descriptive summary:

> "This lesson explained that relationship marketing is an approach to selling that emphasizes developing a close and ongoing connection to customers, listening to their needs, and suggesting products and services that meet those needs. The primary benefits of this approach is that it increases customer satisfaction and repeat business."

Note how the descriptive summary provides key details that learners should remember. If learners missed those points earlier, the descriptive summary offers learners one last chance to grasp them without scrolling back or interacting with a tutor.

End of a Training Program

The end of a training program is your last opportunity to reinforce the key learning points. So you should avoid ending abruptly—finishing the last unit and saying, "Well, that's it folks. Here's the postclass survey."

Instead, offer learners a few moments to reflect on the material taught. Reflecting is not the same as summarizing, something you should do at the end of each unit. If you summarize content at the end of each unit, summarizing it at the end of the program is repetitive. In contrast, reflection helps learners restate the material in a way that is meaningful to them and consider how they might integrate the new skills in their own work.

Course designers and developers use a number of techniques to help learners reflect on the content. Some provide learners with scenarios and ask them what they have learned in the program that specifically helps them respond to the scenarios. Others ask learners to state what lessons they will take away from the program. Still others distribute prestamped envelopes to learners and pieces of paper on which learners write something they hope to do as a result of the training, place it in the envelope, address it to themselves, and seal it. The instructor then mails the sealed envelope to learners at a specified time (between a month and a year after the course). Companies like Mindmarker use software to automate and deepen this postclass reinforcement of training.

Platinum, Silver, and Bronze Types of Projects

Unlike previous chapters in this book, this chapter described methods used to develop silver projects for live and self-study training programs: ones that either have high visibility or are intended for high impact, but not both. Most silver projects include face-to-face classroom training programs and level 2 (moderately complex) online self-study programs.

For platinum projects—face-to-face training programs and level 3 (highly complex) online self-study programs—involve extensive, custom-designed interactions, activities, and videos. Because of their complexity and the level of programming, video, game design, and illustration skills required, most organizations hire outside firms to assist with the development of level 3 materials. Doing so is often more cost-efficient than having all these specialists on staff to work on projects.

More common are bronze projects—live virtual classes and level 1 (least complex) online and workbook-based self-study programs. The processes for developing new programs are the same as described here, but tend to require simpler graphics, video, and programming. But with the rise of inexpensive authoring tools and high-quality recording devices, the quality of bronze programs is often as impressive as that of platinum and silver programs, despite their simplicity. To further simplify and standardize bronze programs, many organizations rely on templates, which allow course designers and developers to reuse designs for slides, screens, and pages, as well as text for similar instructions, rather than having to create materials from scratch.

Silver and bronze projects often involve revisions to existing programs. Sponsors and project managers ask course designers and developers working on revisions to limit changes to the parts that require updates. When updating the materials, though, many course designers and developers overlook revisions to front and back matter, both the entire program and individual units. When revising front and back matter, update the copyright date to reflect the most recent version. Update the table of contents or menu to reflect the newest content. Update the objectives and agenda of the program to reflect new material. Update the summaries to reflect the new material. Update the test or assessment to assess the new material. And update terminology throughout to make sure it reflects new or changed terms.

Getting It Done

The materials that you prepare for a training program depend on whether it is live or self-study. For a live training program, prepare a student guide (vis als, activities, and supplemental materials) and an instructor guide (annotated visuals for delivering content and annotated instructions for administering activities). For a self-study training program, prepare similar material but in such a way that learnerscan use the materials without an instructor.

When opening live and self-study programs, quickly engage learners with the material, even before providing an advance organizer (objectives and preview of the material). In the middle of the program, make sure all instructional materials, and activities directly relate to the objectives of the program, because those that do not can distract learners and make mastering the objectives that much more difficult. And remember to end a program by asking learners to reflect on the material learned and how they will apply it.

Use Exercise 7-1 to guide you through the decisions made when developing the materials for the training program. It provides a checklist of issues you might address.

Exercise 7-1. Guide to Decisions Made While Developing Materials

Preparing Materials for Live Training Programs	
Preparing the student guide	**Preparing the visuals** • Does each visual begin with an assertion? ❑ Yes ❑ No • Does the assertion follow with evidence in the form of an illustration, chart, symbol, or text points? ❑ Yes ❑ No • Do you keep the total number of words on the slide to 30 or fewer? ❑ Yes ❑ No
	Preparing activities and supplemental information • Do the activities begin with a heading that explains their purpose? ❑ Yes ❑ No • Do you provide instructions for completing the activity? ❑ Yes ❑ No • Do you provide hints for handling known trouble spots? ❑ Yes ❑ No • Do you provide forms for recording information during the activity (if needed)? ❑ Yes ❑ No • Do you provide readings, references, and other resources that might extend the training or assist with applying skills on the job? ❑ Yes ❑ No
	Assembling the student guide: • Does it include the following at the beginning of the guide: title page, edition notice, and table of contents? ❑ Yes ❑ No • Does it include the following at the end of the guide: references and evaluation form? ❑ Yes ❑ No • Did you determine how to distribute it? ❑ Print ❑ Digital. • If digital, send by email ❑ or through the learning management system ❑?
Preparing the instructor guide	**Preparing the setup instructions** • For face-to-face classes, did you include instructions for the audiovisual equipment and arrangement of the classroom furniture? ❑ Yes ❑ No • For virtual classes, did you include instructions for uploading slides, setting up interactive questions and polls, and establishing groups (if needed)? ❑ Yes ❑ No • For all classes, did you identify materials needed for demonstrations and learning activities, software and files used in the course, and other materials as needed? ❑ Yes ❑ No • Did you tell instructors where to find these materials and, if needed, how to set them up in the classroom before a session starts? ❑ Yes ❑ No
	Preparing the annotated visuals • Do they include notes rather than a word-for-word script? ❑ Yes ❑ No
	Preparing instructions for administering learning activities: Did you include: • Introductory material? ❑ Yes ❑ No • Annotated instructions, which include instructions for helping learners with known trouble spots? ❑ Yes ❑ No • Description of the solution? ❑ Yes ❑ No • Guide to leading the postactivity debriefing? ❑ Yes ❑ No
	Assembling the instructor guide: • Does it include the following at the beginning of the guide: title page, edition notice, and table of contents? ❑ Yes ❑ No • Is it prepared to be distributed digitally? ❑ Yes ❑ No

Exercise 7-1. Guide to Decisions Made While Developing Materials (continued)

Preparing Materials for Self-Study Training Programs

Did you include the following:
- Title page, screen, or slide? ❑ Yes ❑ No
- Table of contents or menu? ❑ Yes ❑ No
- Edition notice or similar copyright statements? ❑ Yes ❑ No
- Overview of the program? ❑ Yes ❑ No
- Units of the program? ❑ Yes ❑ No
- Lecture, presented as a narrated script or text to be read, which clearly and accurately describes the instructional material using the chosen instructional strategy? ❑ Yes ❑ No
- Activities, which include not only the activity, but also hints for addressing known problem spots and solutions? ❑ Yes ❑ No
- For online programs, storyboards? ❑ Yes ❑ No
- Supplemental information? ❑ Yes ❑ No
- References and other sources of information? ❑ Yes ❑ No
- Test or similar assessment of learning? ❑ Yes ❑ No
- Evaluation form? ❑ Yes ❑ No

8

The Basics of Preparing and Producing Instructional Materials

 What's Inside This Chapter

This chapter explains how to produce the materials used in live and self-study training programs. Specifically, it presents the basics of:

- Preparing instructional materials, including writing text and communicating ideas visually
- Producing the materials, including designing the slides, screens, and pages, preparing complex visuals and audiovisual components, and generating a package of materials to distribute to instructors and learners.

An exercise at the end of this chapter guides you through the process of preparing and producing materials for a project on which you are working.

Aware of the materials needed for the different types of training programs (described in chapter 7), you can now prepare and produce them. Preparing the materials involves writing the instructional text and preparing the visuals that form the key components of a training program. Producing the materials involves combining

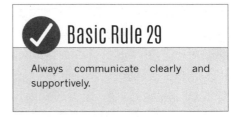

Basic Rule 29

Always communicate clearly and supportively.

all the components onto slides, screens, and pages, creating related media like audio and video clips, and generating a package of materials to distribute to instructors and learners. This chapter explains how course designers and developers do this. Chapter 9 then discusses the review processes that assure the quality of the materials under development.

Preparing Instructional Materials

Preparing instructional materials involves preparing the two key components of training programs: text and visuals. This section suggests some basic tips for preparing each.

Writing Instructional Text

When learners start a training program, they have little to no knowledge of the material. So if the program's objectives are not clear, learners cannot achieve them. Some learners also lack confidence in their ability to master the material. So if the program does not support them properly, they'll drop out before finishing, eliminating their chance of achieving the objectives. This means that the words you choose and messages you convey directly promote (or inhibit) learning, build (or weaken) confidence, and ease (or heighten) frustration. Here are some suggestions for writing instructional text as clearly and supportively as possible.

Limit Material to That Which Pertains to the Learning Objectives

This important point should be stressed throughout the training design, because as you move further into the development process, material not relating to the objectives can more easily slip into the course materials. For example, you might find some interesting material that you want to share with learners or a SME asks you to include an ancillary description as a favor. Despite your good intentions, this material will only distract learners from the objectives and make achieving those objectives all the more difficult.

Use a Positive, Supportive Tone

As you develop training programs, you not only present the instructional material needed to achieve the learning objectives, but also motivate learners to believe they can master them. This belief, in turn, encourages learners to persist in the program until they successfully complete it.

One way to motivate learners is by using a supportive tone, emphasizing the positive, and avoiding assumptions about the way learners feel. Although learners will ultimately make their own assessment of the overall tone of a training program, certain communication tips can help you build a more supportive tone. For example, emphasize the positive and what learners *can* do, not what they *can't*.

Also avoid making assumptions about how learners might respond to the content, particularly assumptions like "This will be easy" and "That's simple," in attempts to lower their anxiety levels. Labeling material as "easy" or "simple" could make learners feel worse if they have difficulty mastering it. Similarly, avoid expressions that presume how learners might feel about the material, such as "Don't you like this?" or "It will make your work easier." Learners might feel differently.

Avoid Technical Jargon and Acronyms

SMEs speak about instructional material using technical jargon, specialized words and phrases that have meaning only to other technical experts in the field. One particularly confusing type of jargon is acronyms: terms created from the first letters of each word in a term. For example, SME (pronounced "smee") is an acronym for subject matter expert.

Using too much jargon and too many acronyms will likely confuse your learners. Most learners struggle to understand them because they have not yet learned the subject, much less the specialized terminology. Furthermore, rather than ask an instructor to define unfamiliar terms—embarrassing in a live program and a complicated task in a self-study one—many learners will pretend to understand, only adding to their confusion. But if they don't understand the terms used in the training program, learners cannot understand the material. And if they cannot understand the material, learners cannot master the objectives of the program.

So avoid unnecessary jargon and acronyms whenever possible. If possible, use plain language equivalents for technical terms. When you cannot, define technical terms and acronyms the first time that you use them in a training program. If you do not use a term again until another unit, define it again in the other unit. Learners might have forgotten the definition or might have skipped the earlier unit. If you only use an acronym once or twice in a unit or course, consider dropping the acronym and spelling out the full term. Doing so minimizes avoidable confusion.

In addition, provide a glossary with instructional materials so learners can quickly find definitions of jargon and acronyms with which they lack familiarity.

Noted

Some SMEs might comment that you'll insult learners by defining technical terms. Ignore this well-intentioned but erroneous advice. Most learners will not speak up if they do not know a term. If you define a term that you feel that many learners already know, begin the definition with comments like "As many of you are already aware" or "To make sure that we're working with similar definitions."

Properly Define Technical Terms and Acronyms

When defining a technical term, avoid all forms of the term in its definition. For example, "Educational technology refers to the technology used in educational settings" is a weak definition because it uses both *educational* and *technology* in the definition. If a learner has difficulty with those two words individually or together, the definition provided would only add to the confusion. Instead, "Educational technology refers to the hardware, software, and thinkware—or processes and conceptual models—used to create instructional programs, with an emphasis on self-study programs taken online" is a much better definition because it avoids any forms of *education* and *technology*.

Define acronyms differently. When introducing an acronym, always spell out the full name and then present the acronym in parentheses after the complete term. Consider again the subject matter expert example:

☒ SME (subject matter expert)
☑ subject matter expert (SME)

Use Examples, Analogies, and Stories

As discussed in chapter 1, adult learners learn best when they can relate to the material. One way to build a relation with the material is through examples, analogies, and stories. Consider these examples:

- To explain how a simple conversation can cause a security breach, a course designer and developer might include stories about conversations that had been overheard and resulted in leaks about upcoming products in the trade press.

- To explain the concept of two-tiered security involving user IDs and passwords in the security course, a course designer and developer might use an analogy to compare user IDs and passwords with the deadbolt locks and security alarm systems used in many homes.

- To prepare learners to conduct their first employee appraisals, an instructor in an introductory course on supervision might relate the experience of the first appraisal she gave to create a connection with learners preparing their own.

Using examples, analogies, and stories offers many benefits. They can make abstract concepts more concrete. They can reinforce learning if you build on them throughout a training program. Seeing examples, analogies, and stories based on the same situation in different units allows learners to easily see relationships among content and, in doing so, reinforces material. (For example, notice how designs for training programs on relationship marketing, security procedures, and supervision keep appearing in this book.)

Clearly Describe Procedures

Many training programs tell learners how to perform a task. How the procedures for performing the task are described makes a significant difference in the ease with which people comprehend and perform the task. When writing procedures, then, consider these specific guidelines:

- State the goal of the procedure as succinctly as possible. A clear heading, if used, will often suffice.

- If readers need knowledge, supplies, or assistance to perform the procedure, state that information in a "Read Me First" section, which precedes the procedure. In that way, when they start performing the procedure, they have the resources needed.

- Provide an estimate of the time needed to complete the procedure—and estimate a little bit more time than the average user needs to complete the procedure. If users complete the procedure in less time, they will feel a sense of success.

- Write procedures as numbered lists, which tells readers the sequence for performing the steps. Readers also recall the step numbers when leaving the text to perform tasks. Presenting tasks as a paragraph makes following along while performing the task difficult.

- Because users can handle only a limited amount of information at any given time, limit the length to 10 steps. If your procedure has more steps, break them into "mini-procedures" within the larger procedures. If you use a numbered list (1, 2, 3) for the main procedure, use a lettered list (a, b, c) for the mini-procedures.

- As with writing tasks, limit each step in a procedure to one task. If the step has several tasks, break the step into several steps or write a mini-procedure. Real-world experience indicates that users stop reading as soon as they encounter the action to be performed in a step.
- Present conditional information as a clause at the beginning of a step; do not place it after the action verb.
- Use the imperative—that is, begin with an action verb and tell readers what to do. Research shows that users read these types of directions faster than ones that do not begin with actions (see Van der Meij, Karreman, and Steehouder, 2009, for a summary of research on writing instructions).
- Introduce "must-know" terminology and concepts in the procedure, rather than in the "Read Me First" section. Learners will forget the term by the time you use it in the procedure.
- Tell learners when they have completed the procedure. When doing so, describe the results of successful completion as well as unsuccessful results that can be anticipated. Without explicitly telling learners that they have completed the procedure, they might not realize on their own that they have done so.

Carefully Use Lists

Often the best way to emphasize key points is through the use of bulleted and numbered lists. Lists offer several benefits. Because they appear to learners as if they are a series of separate paragraphs, lists increase the likelihood that people who skim content will see the points on the list. When skimming, readers typically focus on the first line or two of a paragraph then move to the next.

Lists also help learners see relationships, especially the sequence of tasks in a procedure or the unfolding events in the past.

To make sure you receive the most value from lists, consider these specific suggestions:

- Choose the right type of list. When the items on the list follow a set sequence (such as tasks in a procedure or events in history), use a numbered list. When you can change the order of items on a list without changing the meaning, use a bulleted list.
- Whenever you use lists, make sure you have at least two list items (such as two or more bullet points or two or more numbered steps in a procedure). Otherwise, use a paragraph. A single bullet point looks odd, as though something's missing.

- When presenting bullet points, use parallel grammatical construction. Parallel grammatical construction means that each bullet point begins with the same type of word (verb or noun). When one bullet point follows a different structure, it calls attention to itself and distracts learners from the message at hand. Learners focus, instead, on the question, "Why does this bullet point look weird?" For example, consider the third bullet item in Figure 8-1. It looks like it does not belong to the list.

Figure 8-1. Failure to Use Parallel Construction Makes for an Odd-Looking Slide

Goals for the coming year

- Grow 10.3 percent next year
- Increase sales
- Costs

Reinforce Learning Through Repetition

Using the same phrases and terms throughout a program builds familiarity with new concepts. For example, when introducing a concept at the beginning of a unit, referring to it during the unit, and summarizing it at the end of the unit, use the same phrases. Using the same phrases reinforces that you are trying to make the same point.

Communicating Ideas Visually

Visuals play a central role in training materials. First, most organizations present the instructional material in training programs through a screen, whether projecting a slide in a classroom or presenting material on screen in an online course. Screens are all essentially visual media in which images—rather than text or narration—carry the primary responsibility for communicating messages. Words merely support the visuals, clarifying what is not evident in the image. Second, visuals often communicate ideas and concepts in less space than words. Writers need at least a good paragraph or two to provide a basic description of computers. A picture can convey most of that definition in the space of a paragraph; a video or animation can convey all of the information in about the same physical space as the picture. Third, in some instances, visuals are easier to understand than text, and learners remember images better than words. So whenever possible and appropriate, consider whether images would be more effective than text in conveying an idea.

Communicating visually through pictures and similar images presents a challenge to most course designers and developers, who are trained primarily to communicate through words. Furthermore, many course designers and developers believe they have to be able to draw to effectively use visuals. This is not true. Instead, course designers and developers merely need to be able to choose the right type of image and provide sufficient instructions for a professional illustrator or graphic designer to prepare that image.

When might a visual be helpful? Table 8-1 suggests some specific situations in which you should always think about using a visual to communicate instructional material and the type of visual to consider using.

Table 8-1. Situations in Which You Should Consider Using Visuals to Communicate Instructional Material

Situation	Type of Image
Reporting financial figures	If you are showing relationships of parts to a whole (like the division of a budget), use a pie chart. If you are showing financial figures over time, use a bar chart.
Reporting trends over time	Use a histogram, which uses a single point to represent the financial figures for each point in time.
Showing products	For presales efforts such as marketing, use a photograph. For postsales efforts (like troubleshooting), use a line drawing, which is easier to follow for the purposes of technical training because it only shows the most relevant details. Photographs show extraneous details, which can distract learners.
Presenting a sequence of events or steps	Use a flowchart, which shows how one step or event relates to the next.
Showing relationships	Use an organizational chart or a map.

Producing Instructional Materials

With text and visuals prepared, you can begin production. As noted earlier, production is the process in which you create materials to distribute to instructors and learners. It involves three major tasks: first, designing slides, screens, and pages; second, preparing complex visuals and audiovisual components; and third, generating packages of materials to distribute to instructors and learners.

Note that, because most course designers and developers prepare drafts of programs as slides, screens, and pages, this section describes the basics of designing these pieces first, even though course designers and developers do not finalize the designs until after completion of the complex visuals and audiovisual recordings.

Designing Slides, Screens, and Pages

Course designers and developers present their training programs as slides, screens, and pages. Live training programs usually take the form of slides, though pages can be used to present activities and supplemental information. Self-study training programs use all three. Some online tutorials rely on slides for the slidecasts. Other online tutorials are built around screens. Some activities and supplemental information in these programs might take the form of pages. All three combine text and visuals, with slides and screens sometimes also incorporating audiovisual components.

This section describes how to design each. It starts with general design tips for all three. Then it describes specific suggestions for designing your own slides (building on the suggestions in chapter 7), screens, and pages. It closes with some additional considerations for designing these components, including what to do if you work from templates.

General Tips

To ensure that programs best facilitate learning, follow some general suggestions regarding the grid, blank space, headings, and type when designing slides, screens, and pages. Subsequent sections in this chapter provide specific suggestions for designing slides, screens, and pages.

 Basic Rule 30

Design plays a significant role in the preparation of slides, screens, and pages because a broad range of research in cognitive psychology, educational technology, and professional communication (summarized by Hartley, 2013, and van der Geest and Spyridakis, 2000) has shown that different design choices affect the ease with which learners go through the program and that, in turn, influences their success. For example, consistency in arranging materials on the slide, screen, or page reduces the mental effort learners need to move from one frame to another or from one unit to another. The spacing of material on the slides, screens, and pages as well as the choice of type can either facilitate learning or cause fatigue. If sufficiently fatigued, learners might choose to leave training programs before completing them, especially optional self-study programs.

Become familiar with the basic grid. Slides, screens, and pages are all designed around a basic arrangement, called a grid. Figure 8-2 shows a sample grid. The grid has these elements:

- Margins, or the space around the edges of the slide, screen, and page.
- Basic navigational components, which usually appear at the top or bottom of the grid, or on one of the sides. These navigational components, such as sequence numbers (slides and pages) and progress bars (screens), help learners determine where they are in the program. Headings on slides, *breadcrumbs* (brief statements showing the unit and lesson within the program) on screens, and running headers on pages help learners determine their place within the program. They also help learners easily jump among parts of the program. Buttons and links on screens and tabs on pages facilitate these jumps. In most instances, the software used to generate the slides, screens, and pages lets you create navigational components once and automatically places them thereafter.
- Content area, which is the space in the middle of the slide, screen, or page where you place the text, visuals, and recordings of the instructional material.

Figure 8-2. General Grid (Not Drawn to Proportion)

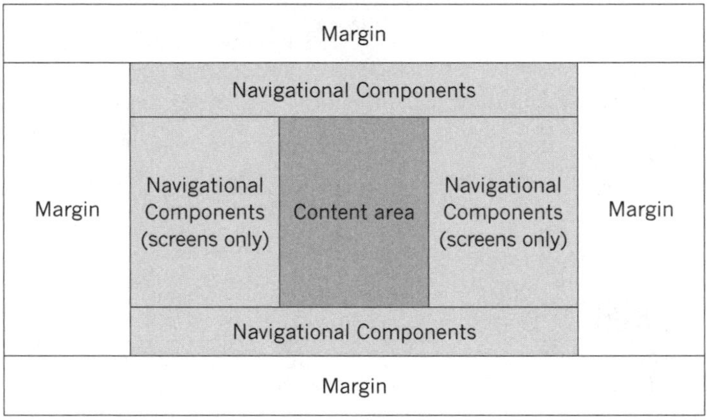

Leave some blank (white) space. Blank space refers to empty portions of the slide, screen, or page where no text or visuals appear. (Some people refer to this as white space, especially when talking about pages.) Blank space provides readers a rest from long blocks of text. It visually separates items, such as pictures from text, one paragraph from another, and headings from the passages that follow. It also serves as margins, which provide a border of sorts for the slide, screen, or page.

Studies suggest that you should leave at least 25 percent of the slide, screen, or page as blank space to facilitate easy reading. (Note if you plan to translate the training program into another language, experts also advise leaving another 25 percent blank—for a total of 50 percent—for the translated text, especially if you write the original in English. Some other languages need more words to make the same point.)

To make sure that slides, screens, and pages have sufficient blank space, you should:

- leave margins at the top and bottom and on the sides
- leave space between the central block of content and the navigational components
- leave space between blocks of material
- indent the first line of a paragraph or leave a blank line between paragraphs
- leave some space between a heading and the text that follows.

Also use your eye to determine whether blank space is needed. If a slide, screen, or page looks a little full with text, add blank space to the area that looks crowded.

Use headings. Headings are brief statements placed before a section of material that describe what's to follow. On visually based materials like slides, headings state the purpose of the slide or screen. On text-based materials like the exercises and supplemental information in live training programs, text screens in online tutorials, and workbooks in general, headings state the purpose of the text that follows the heading and help learners easily find information when scanning pages for specific material.

Course designers and developers use different heading levels to help learners distinguish the importance of various sections. The lower the heading number, the more significant the section that follows. Heading 1 identifies a unit or chapter and generally has the largest and boldest appearance of all the headings in the document. Heading 2 identifies a major section within a unit or chapter, Heading 3 a section within a major section, and Heading 4 a subsection within a section. Use the same formatting for headings to identify sections at the same level in the hierarchy and do so consistently throughout the learning program.

> ### 💬 Noted
>
> Most word processing and desktop publishing systems let you enter headings according to their level by style or formatting the heading text. For example, in Microsoft Word you can assign a style by highlighting the text to include in the heading, then clicking on the chosen style in the button bar at the top of the screen. Similarly, markup languages like HTML and XML provide special codes or tags for indicating different levels of headings.

Use type properly. Much research (which James Hartley nicely summarizes in *Designing Instructional Text*) has focused on the impact of typography on reading, which has resulted in general guidelines for using it. First, consider these general concepts in typography, as they underlie the guidelines:

- A typeface is a particular look or design for the set of characters, and a font is a complete set of characters in one typeface.
- Type is classified as serif and sans serif. According to Alred, Brusaw, and Oliu (2000), "Typography is characterized by the presence or absence of serifs. . . . A serif is a 'small projection at end of a stroke of a letter.'" Serif fonts contain serifs; sans serif fonts do not. (Note that the word *sans* means without.) For an example, see Table 8-2.
- Size of type is stated in units called *points*. One point is 1/72 of an inch. Guidelines for type vary by situation. Figure 8-3 shows examples of type size.

Table 8-2. Some Basic Serif and Sans Serif Typefaces

Serif	Sans Serif
Century Schoolbook	Arial
Georgia	Helvetica
Palatino Linotype	Tahoma
Times New Roman	Verdana

Figure 8-3. Examples of Type Size

Point Size

- Points are a printer's measurement system
  - 1 point = 1/72 of an inch
  - 6 points = 1 pica

- Examples

word 11   word 18   word 24   word 32

When using type, consider these guidelines:

- Limit the number of fonts on a slide, screen, or page. Because different fonts can clash with one another for attention, only use two fonts on a slide, screen, and page: one for the headings, the other for body text.
- Make sure that the two fonts coordinate nicely. The font for headings should coordinate well with the font chosen for body text. For example, if you choose a sans serif font for one, choose a serif font for the other.
- Appropriately use emphasis type. Although emphasis type such as boldface and italics helps call attention to text, publishing convention limits the use of each to particular instances so that their emphasis really stands out. Excessive use of emphasis type works counter to the original intentions: rather than calling attention to text, it draws attention away from it. Table 8-3 suggests the appropriate uses for the most common forms of emphasis type.
- Choose an appropriate type size. On screens and pages, use 10–point type. On slides, use 40–48 point type for headings and 24–40 for body text.

Table 8-3. When to Use Emphasis Type

Boldface	Use for headings. Note that the term *headings* is broadly defined here and includes headings and captions for charts and tables, as well as notes, cautions, and warnings. Avoid using bold to highlight a word in a paragraph or the first word of each item on a list as doing so can look "busy" to readers.
Italics	Use to denote the titles of published works, such as books, periodicals, and films, such as *TD* or *Informal Learning Basics*). Also use to identify words appropriated from other languages and that have not become standard English (such as *détente*).
<u>Underscore</u>	Use to identify hyperlinks. Underscores are so widely used to identify hyperlinks that many learners automatically click on underscored text, regardless of whether the text itself actually links to anything.
ALL CAPS	Use for abbreviations and acronyms only. Using all caps to emphasize text fails on two levels. First, learners have more difficulty reading text that is all uppercase than they do with mixed-case letters because learners have a difficult time distinguishing one capital letter from another. Second, learners usually perceive all capitalized type as being yelled at.

With these general guidelines regarding the grid, blank space, headings, and type in mind, consider specific guidelines for designing slides, screens, and pages.

Designing Slides

Slides form the basic unit of live training programs—both face-to-face and online—and for tutorials created from slidecasts. To design visible, legible, and clear slides, consider these guidelines:

 Basic Rule 31

Design slides to be visible, legible, and clear. *Visible* means that learners in face-to-face classes can see the letters and images on the slide in the back row of the classroom or at their computers with requiring any magnification. *Legible* means that the letters and images on the slide are easily deciphered by learners. *Clear* means that learners can decipher the message on the first read-through.

Become familiar with the basic grid. The general grid presented earlier is adapted for slides as shown in Figure 8-4. The content area has two major sections: the assertion, where you place the sentence that provokes discussion or narration, and the evidence, where you place evidence that illuminates the assertion.

Figure 8-4. General Grid of a Slide

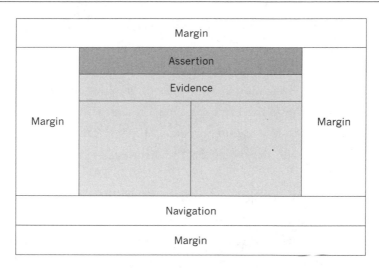

Because slides do not let learners easily jump to other parts, the navigation parts are, for the most part, removed, except at the bottom. Many course designers and developers place a slide number there; others also include the date.

Limit the amount of text on a slide. The text on a slide is intended to serve as a reminder of key points, not a transcript of the lecture, even in slidecasts. So on any one slide, limit the total number of words to 30–35. That number includes all words—both in the assertion and the supporting evidence.

Use capitalization carefully. For headings, capitalize the first letter of each word except articles (such words as *a, an,* and *the*) and prepositions (such words as *of, by,* and *to*). For each bullet point, capitalize the first letter of the first word. Do not capitalize other words except for proper names of people, organizations, departments, products, and countries. Do not capitalize generic department names (such as sales and engineering) or the generic names of products (such as computers and pharmaceuticals). For example, use Don Tremblay, vice president of sales, rather than Don Tremblay, Vice President of Sales.

Use a legible type size. Most type for reading is between 10 points and 14 points. However, for slides there are different recommended guidelines for headings (40–48 points), bullets (32–40 points), and captions and callouts (24–32 points).

Use contrast to distinguish text from the background. A high contrast is one in which learners can easily distinguish the letters and images on the slide. The sharper the contrast between the letters and images and the background, the easier learners can read them. The ideal contrast for most slides is black text on a white background.

The only major exception is for slides intended to be used in face-to-face classrooms that will be darkened during the program. In such cases, reverse the plan: Use light type (white or cream) on a dark background (such as black or deep blue).

Carefully use animation. Animation is a sequence of graphics on a single slide that appears to learners as if the images move. You can use animation with visuals directly projected from a computer during a live face-to-face training program, and you can usually do so in live virtual classrooms and online tutorials, depending on the software. Some common animation techniques include:

- Show movement in a process.
- Display text one line at a time on a slide to help focus a live discussion on one point at a time. If all of the points were to appear, learners might jump ahead and skip some important intermediate issues.
- Transition between slides. This technique can visually signal a message to learners, such as "We're starting a new section," or "Here's an example."

 Noted

Watch out for overuse of animation; it can quickly become distracting or annoying. Annoying uses of animation include noisy animation, like swoosh sounds used in transitions, typing sounds used when displaying lines one at a time, the overuse of displaying text one line at a time (which quickly loses its power to focus discussions), and transitions among slides.

Designing Screens
Screens form the basic unit of some types of online tutorials, especially tutorials with moderately complex interactions.

✔ Basic Rule 32

Design screens so learners can easily read them. Research, such as that compiled by van der Geest and Spyridakis (2000), suggests that reading a passage online might take longer than reading on a printed page and that retention is slightly lower. Also design screens so learners can easily move to the next screen because if they cannot figure out how to do so, they will drop out of the program.

To design easy-to-read-and-navigate screens, consider these guidelines:

Become familiar with the basic grid. The general grid presented in Figure 8-2 accurately represents the grid for a screen. Note, however, that because the margins and navigational components do not change, learners tend to focus all of their attention on the content area of the screen. And although a screen can be scrollable—that is, presents material that does not appear on the screen until learners hit the Page Down or arrow keys or swipe downward—many course designers and developers prefer to design fixed screens whenever possible. Past experience suggests that learners often do not scroll down on tutorial screens and thus miss the material that is "below the fold" (not visible when the screen first appears).

Design standard formats for recurring screens. Although the material on each screen is unique, the type of material is not. Some screens present material as text, with graphics illustrating the key points. Some screens instruct learners to answer questions and later provide feedback on the responses. Some screens introduce a unit, some provide a menu to the content, and others summarize a completed unit. Designing recurring formats establishes expectations of what will appear on the screen.

Use a legible type size. Most type for reading is between 8 and 14 points:

- For body type, use a **12-point sans serif font.** Research such as that compiled by Hartley (2013) and van der Geest and Spyridakis (2000) suggests that, on a screen, a sans serif font is easier to read than a serif one.
- For heading 4, use ***12-point bold and italic type.***
- For heading 3, use **12-point bold type.**
- For heading 2, use **14-point bold type.**
- For heading 1, use **16-point bold type.**

Justify text on the left margin only. Justification refers to the alignment of text on the margin. *Left justification* means text is aligned to the left margin, *right justification* to the right margin.

Centering text places text equally distant from either margin. You can also justify text on both the left and right margins (*full justification*). Margins that are not justified are called *ragged.*

Although many choices exist, only justify text on the left margin. Because readers scan documents along the left margin, they tend to miss anything placed in the center, even headings. Also, avoid using full justification. To justify the text on both margins, the computer either stretches the letters or adds extra space between words. Either way, the type looks strange and interferes with reading.

Use contrast to distinguish text from the background. A high contrast is one in which learners can easily distinguish the letters and images on the screen. The sharper the contrast between letters and images, and the background, the easier learners can read them. The ideal contrast for most screens is black text on a white background (same as slides).

Leave headings and body text in black unless they indicate links. Not only do black and white provide the strongest contrast, but experience with computer and mobile device users suggests that learners perceive headings and text in colors other than black as hyperlinks. Many users even click on the text and expect the system to display a new page. To prevent such confusion, only use color for text or headings when presenting a hyperlink.

Carefully use pop-up windows. Pop-up windows are windows that appear when learners click on a particular link. Pop-ups let the system display material on top of related material. Examples include clicking on a word and displaying its definition or clicking on a part of an image and seeing a blown-up image. When used sparingly, pop-ups can enhance the learning experience. When used extensively, pop-ups annoy learners, so much so that many learners turn off the ability of their browsers to display them.

Designing Pages

To design pages for easy reading, consider these guidelines:

Become familiar with the basic grid. The general grid presented in Figure 8-2 is adapted for a page as shown in Figure 8-5. Consider carefully the information provided in navigational components. For example, some organizations include the page number and the name of the training program on left-hand pages and the page number and the name of the unit on right-hand pages. Also decide whether to place the navigational components at the top, bottom, or split between the two. And keep in mind the size of margins on "inside" pages (that is, between one page and its facing page—right margins for left-hand pages and left margins for right-hand pages). They should be slightly bigger than the ones on the outside so that the document can be placed in a binder without "losing" material. Otherwise, the words on the page might get caught in the binding.

Basic Rule 33

Like screens, design pages for easy reading. Research, such as that summarized by Schriver (1996), shows that strong designs of pages help learners easily find information and, when they read it, minimize the fatigue that might arise from extensive reading.

Figure 8-5. Grid for a Page

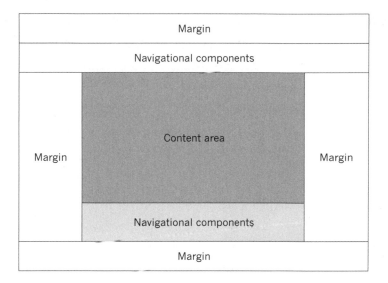

Plan a clean, simple layout. Layout refers to the arrangement of elements on the page. Thoughtful arrangement of them can simplify the task of learning. Through its ability to attract and maintain attention, layout helps learners distinguish the most important material and draws attention to material that learners might overlook. Of course, incompletely thought-out layouts can have the opposite effect.

When designing pages, place the most important material at the upper right corner of a right-hand page. This is the first place that learners look for content when opening a two-page spread of a book. For this reason, you might notice that most books start new sections on a right-hand page.

Design pages for "scanability." One of the challenges learners face when using printed materials is locating information. Learners scan the running headers to find a general location and headings to find specific locations.

Design standard layouts for recurring types of pages. As with screens, certain types of pages recur in instructional materials. Some examples of recurring types of pages include first and last pages of units, pages that only present text, pages that present text and graphics, pages with additional information, and pages with exercises and, perhaps, related feedback. So as recommended for screens, prepare standard layouts for recurring types of pages. (Note how standard layouts are used in this book for the opening sections of each chapter, and the boxes *Basic Rules, Think About This,* and *Noted.*)

Use a legible type. Research such as that summarized by Schriver (1996) suggests that a serif font is easier to read on a page than a sans serif one. (Note that this is the opposite of the recommendation for screens.) Also use the same type sizes for pages as for screens.

- For body type, use a 12-point font.
- For heading 4, use ***12-point bold and italic type.***
- For heading 3, use **12-point bold type.**
- For heading 2, use **14-point bold type.**
- For heading 1, use **16-point bold type.**

Working With Templates

As noted earlier in this book, templates are like fill-in-the-blank forms that let you quickly start preparing a new training program. The template encodes the layout (organization of information) of the slide, screen, or page, as well as its margins, type fonts and sizes, navigation, and other design features. Many organizations prepare templates for recurring slides, screens, and pages to ensure that training programs share a visual appearance and appropriately reflect the organizational brand. Organizations also use templates to increase efficiency in designing and developing training programs. By using existing and proven templates, organizations minimize time spent on the visual design.

Basic Rule 34

If you are asked to work with a template, start by familiarizing yourself with its key features (such as location of navigational elements, fonts, and heading structure) and the types of recurring slides, screens, or pages. Also find out who can answer questions about the template and who handles any changes you may have to it.

Preparing Complex Visuals and Audiovisual Components

The next production task involves preparing complex visuals and audiovisual components. As noted earlier, preparing a training program involves drafting slides, screens, and pages. Although the text is fully written at that time, the visuals are only sketched—not prepared in a form that can be presented to learners. After the slides are prepared and the text approved, preparation of finished visuals—that is, turning those sketches into finished images and animations—begins. Recording of narration that accompanies the slides also occurs at this time. This section describes how to produce the complex visuals that were sketched earlier and how to record the audiovisual sequences that were drafted earlier.

Preparing Complex Visuals

Producing complex visuals involves preparing final versions of the visuals sketched in early drafts of the training program. Illustrators or graphic designers can produce complex visuals—illustrations and three-dimensional drawings—using an illustration application like Adobe Illustrator, and you can later combine the resulting digital images with the text and save them for future use. Illustrators and graphic designers can also modify visuals prepared beforehand. For example, they can add and remove parts of the visual and crop it (cut off part of it and change its size and proportions). This requires substantially less time than starting from scratch.

When it comes to photos, many course designers and designers—especially those on a tight budget—take their own, often with their smartphones. But course designers and developers still hire photographers for the high-visibility projects that require particular shots, excellent lighting, intentional placement of items in the photo, and other details that require the skill of a professional. If the photos are going to include people, course designers and developers sometimes hire models, which ultimately keeps costs down. When using amateurs, photographers often have to reshoot several times to get an acceptable image.

✅ Basic Rule 35

Regardless of whether you use a photographer or hire models, whenever you use images of people in a training program, you need to receive their written permission to do so. Use a model release form to record it, and keep the form in a safe place.

Illustrators and graphic designers can also help you correct imperfections in the photos. They can use photo editing software like Adobe Photoshop to retouch the photo and remove unnecessary details like an arm seemingly not attached to any person in the photograph, change the image size, remove blemishes, and enhance the colors.

Recording Audiovisual Components

Audiovisual components, such as slidecast narrations and other audio and video recordings, can be complex to produce. Slidecast narrations are often easier to produce than other types of recordings because the software used to create and edit them was specifically designed for use by course designers and developers.

To produce a slidecast follow these steps. First, become familiar with the software, such as Camtasia, Articulate (all varieties), and Adobe Captivate, for recording the slidecast and make one or two practice recordings. Although they work on the same computer on which you display the slides, the different slidecast applications have unique means for identifying which part of the screen to show in the recorded visual and for starting and stopping the recording. After you record the slidecast, these applications require that you convert the "raw" recordings into an application-specific video format, such as the common MP4 format. So become familiar with the different formats available and determine which meets your needs.

Second, if you have a script and prepared slides, ask someone to read through the script, even if you plan to record your own narration. This allows you to hear how the words sound coming from another person. Follow along on a printed copy and note any places that sound awkward or seem unclear; adjust them later. For example, you might rewrite a sequence after the reader complains that it has too many difficult-to-pronounce words or you might rewrite mispronounced words phonetically. If someone else narrates the slidecast, this step can help avoid having the narrator stumble through reading the script.

Third, after revising the script, practice the narration with the slides. If you narrate your own slidecast, do this yourself. If someone else like a SME narrates the slidecast, schedule a time to practice. When practicing, focus on the match between slides and narration. Make sure that the instructions to advance slides occur when you want the next slide to appear and that animations and other special images appear when planned. Also focus on the narration again during the rehearsal. As with the practice round, prepare to make minor adjustments to sequences read with difficulty. Practice a second time with the revised script to ensure familiarization with the text.

Fourth, find a quiet place where no one can interrupt you and no one can hear background sounds, like telephones ringing and voices from other offices. A meeting room, with a "Recording, Do Not Disturb" sign posted on the door often serves the purpose. If available, a private studio offers the ideal environment.

Fifth, record the narration. If you make mistakes, stop and start the recording again, either from the beginning or from a specific slide.

Sixth, if necessary, edit the recording. You can remove mistakes, like sudden starts and stops, clearing the throat, and lengthy, unplanned silences. You can also reorganize the program by moving one section to another.

Basic Rule 36

Production is about attending to details, which vary depending on the nature of the materials.

Seventh, after editing, produce a digital file of the recording. Use a file format that plays on most devices, such as MP4.

Eighth, test the file on different devices (such as computers and tablets) and with different browsers to make sure the video works on the devices on which you expect learners to view the video.

Ninth, after testing and making any necessary technical changes, save the file in a safe place and make at least one backup copy, to make sure you do not lose the work.

Although they follow a similar process, more complex audio and video recordings usually require outside assistance. If you plan to record full video—with recordings of people (either workers in your organization or professional actors)—contact a professional director. The director can work with you to finalize plans for the video, prepare storyboards of the video (much like storyboards produced for draft training programs), and oversee all aspects of production, from reserving recording space and acquiring special recording equipment and props to hiring talent, including producers, audio and video engineers and editors, actors, and production assistants.

Generating a Package of Materials to Distribute to Instructors and Learners

Production—the process of preparing course materials for duplication—and related printing are relatively simple processes but involve numerous details. Missing a detail can cause significant problems, including delays in completing the training program.

The actual process of production involves combining the produced components into master copies, and then duplicating the master copies. Specifically, production involves copyediting text; combining the text, graphics, and audiovisual segments into a single file; verifying that online components work as intended, making a backup of the master copy/the backup and storing in a safe place; and sending the master; copy to print or publishing it online.

Copyediting Text

Copyediting, one of the topics addressed in more detail in chapter 9, is the process of marking text for final typesetting. Copyediting begins after your sponsor has approved all of the text and images, and released them for publication. A copyeditor looks for grammatical and stylistic errors, verifies that copyrighted material and trademark are used properly, and makes sure that the production staff has adequate instructions for producing a communication product.

Combining Text, Graphics, and Audiovisual Segments Into Master Files

With the text finalized, you can integrate it with the visuals and audiovisual segments produced earlier in a single master file. First, determine which file or files will serve as the master file and what file format it should follow. Live training programs typically have two master files: one with the slides and instructor's notes (usually prepared in a presentation graphics program) and another with the activities and supplemental information (usually prepared in a word processor). Online tutorials with slidecasts typically have several master files for the videos, exercises, and offline activities and supplemental information. Level 2 and 3 e-learning tutorials typically have one master file for each unit. Workbooks typically have one master file, usually prepared with a word processor or desktop publishing program.

Second, integrate completed visuals into the master files at the exact location where you would like them to appear.

Third, check and correct any pagination problems with word processing and desktop publishing files. For example, on slides and screens, does all of the material appear on the screen or is scrolling required to see everything? If scrolling is required, did you intend to allow scrolling? If not, material will need to be adjusted so it all appears on the screen at one time.

If the design calls for all new units in printed materials to start on a right-hand page, make sure that's where they appear. If you start each unit in a workbook with the page number X-1 (where *X* is the number of the chapter), then make sure the first page of chapter 1 is 1-1 and the first page of chapter 2 is 2-1.

Fourth, generate the table of contents. This is only needed for printed materials; online materials automatically generate a table of contents. Make sure that your word processing or desktop publishing program has included every page and that it assigned the correct page numbers in the table of contents. Additionally, make sure that each page has the proper page number and running header or footer.

You especially need to perform this double-check if your desktop publishing program is automatically generating tables of contents, running headers or footers, and indexes. Glitches in the software often result in tables of contents with page numbers that are off by one page and running headers that do not get "picked up" by the software.

Verifying That Online Components Work as Intended

For all online components, verify that they work as you planned by performing three technical tests: a functional test, a system test, and a load test. A functional test verifies that all of the links, quiz and test questions, feedback, and other interactive elements work as planned. For example, if a learner answers *a* to a multiple-choice question and the answer is correct, verify whether the system responds accordingly. If not, fix the problem before proceeding. A system test makes sure that under normal operating conditions (such as running the program in a browser on a computer with six tabs open) the training program does not interfere with the operations of other programs on the device. A load test checks to see how many learners can take the same program at the same time on the network. It assesses the impact on the overall performance of the program (for example, does the course run more slowly after 10 learners connect to it?) and when it causes the system to crash (for example, does the system crash when 100 learners attempt to take the program at one time?).

Making a Backup of the Master Files

Make a copy of the master file, which should include both the source file and a printout, and store the copy in a safe place. If anything should happen to the master copy, you have a duplicate. This copy also serves as the basis for any future revision. The

Basic Rule 37

Make backup copies throughout the development process to avoid losing work.

printout provides additional protection. Most organizations also have a formal location for these copies of master files so that others in the organization can use them should the need arise.

Sending the Master Copy to the Printer or Publishing It Online

If you plan to formally print materials for learners, you need to send the master copy to the printer, which might require that you provide additional information and markups. After receiving the printed copies, prepare a package that includes a copy of the visuals, student materials (including the student guide you produced and other materials that might be distributed to learners), and instructor guide. Give copies of this package to the administrators who will support the program and the instructors who will teach it.

If you plan to distribute the materials online (including materials that you expect learners to print themselves), you need to publish them online. Most organizations publish training materials through a learning management system, which automates many tasks in administering training groups. In a learning management system, most training programs have their own space. When publishing materials for a program, you upload the materials to that space. If you are providing several different types of materials—different videos, files with copies of slides, other files with supplemental information—you can arrange the materials in the order in which you prefer learners use them. Most learning management systems also let you add some additional text directions for learners.

Note that you can also distribute printed materials like workbooks and exercises and supplemental information through learning management systems. You can post the PDF file, which learners can download and, if desired, print.

Platinum, Silver, and Bronze Types of Projects

The preparation and production processes described in this chapter pertain to silver and bronze projects, not platinum ones. The projects typically involve either live training programs or self-study programs consisting of slidecasts or workbooks (or both). In these types of projects, illustrations are adapted from other sources, and many of the photographs are taken by the course designer and developer or another member of the project team.

Some silver and bronze projects involve revisions to existing training programs. In such instances, focus on ensuring consistency between new and existing materials. The new material should use the same writing and visual communication styles and same terminology as the earlier version. Similarly, the designs of new slides, screens, and pages should be indistinguishable from slides, screens, and pages in the original program. Even minor inconsistencies can distract learners.

If you are developing a new platinum project, you would probably use more original video and illustrations and professionally shot photographs, and develop complex interactions. For each, you would work with specialists such as illustrators, graphic designers, video directors, and programmers to help you prepare and produce the program.

Getting It Done

Preparing instructional materials involves writing the instructional text and communicating ideas visually. Producing instructional materials is the process that combines these components onto slides, screens, and pages, creates related media like videos and audio recordings, and generates a package of materials to distribute to instructors and learners.

After preparing the materials for a training project on which you are working, use Exercise 8-1 to review them. It provides a checklist of issues you might address and activities you need to consider, and helps you keep track of the many details involved in production.

Exercise 8-1. A Checklist for Preparing and Producing Instructional Materials

Writing instructional text	❑ Limit material to that which pertains to the learning objectives ❑ Use a positive, supportive tone ❑ Avoid technical jargon and acronyms ❑ Properly define technical terms and acronyms ❑ Use examples, analogies, and stories ❑ Clearly describe procedures ❑ Carefully use lists ❑ Reinforce learning through repetition
Communicating ideas visually	❑ Report financial figures with a pie chart ❑ Report financial data and trends over time with bar charts ❑ Show product presales with photographs and postsales with line drawings ❑ Show relationships with organizational charts or maps
Following general design guidelines	❑ Become familiar with the basic grid ❑ Leave some blank space (at least 25 percent) ❑ Use headings to signal learners about upcoming content ❑ Only use two fonts, one for headings and another for body text ❑ Appropriately use emphasis type

(continued)

Exercise 8-1. A Checklist for Preparing and Producing Instructional Materials (continued)

Designing slides	❑ Design slides to be legible and clear ❑ Become familiar with the basic grid ❑ Limit the amount of text on a slide to 30–35 words ❑ Use capitalization carefully ❑ Use a legible type size ❑ Use contrast to distinguish text from the background ❑ Carefully use animation
Designing screens	❑ Design screens to be legible and clear ❑ Become familiar with the basic grid ❑ Determine whether the content area should be scrollable ❑ Design standard formats for recurring types of screens ❑ Use a legible type size ❑ Justify text on the left margin only ❑ Use black text on a white background ❑ Carefully use pop-up windows
Designing pages	❑ Design pages to be legible and clear ❑ Determine where to place navigational components and what information to include ❑ Plan a clean, simple layout ❑ Design pages for "scanability" ❑ Design standard layouts for recurring types of pages ❑ Use a serif font for body text and sans serif font for headings ❑ Use a legible type size
Working with templates	❑ Become familiar with the key features of the template ❑ Become familiar with recurring types of slides, screens, or pages that have templates ❑ Find out who can answer questions about the template and make changes to it
Preparing complex visuals	❑ Prepare original illustrations and three-dimensional drawings ❑ Update existing illustrations ❑ Take and retouch photos ❑ Ensure that each person appearing in a photo has signed a model release form
Preparing audiovisual sequences	❑ Become familiar with the software for recording the slidecast and make one or two practice recordings ❑ Ask someone to read through the narration to ensure its readability ❑ Revise the narration if necessary ❑ Practice the narration with the slides again ❑ Prepare for the recording by finding a quiet place ❑ Record the narration ❑ Edit the recording if necessary ❑ Produce a digital file ❑ Test the file on different devices ❑ Save the file and at least one backup copy in a safe place
Producing programs	❑ Copyedit the text ❑ Combine the text, graphics, and audiovisual segments into a single file ❑ Verify that online components work as intended ❑ Make a backup copy of the master, and store it in a safe place ❑ Send the master copy to print or publish it online

9

The Basic Quality Checks for Training Programs

 What's Inside This Chapter

This chapter introduces the basics of evaluating a draft training program to assess its probable effectiveness and the related process of revising drafts. The goal of these activities is improving the likelihood that a training program will achieve its objectives. Specifically, this chapter describes:

- Formative evaluation, the process of evaluating draft training programs
- The three basic types of formative evaluation: pilot tests, technical reviews, and editorial and production reviews
- The basics of revision, including how to respond to feedback and revise materials.

An exercise at the end of this chapter helps you plan the formative evaluation for a project on which you are working.

What Is Formative Evaluation?

One of the key challenges of preparing a training program is making sure that it will accomplish the objectives for which you developed it. Assessing the effectiveness of a training program while it is under development is called *formative evaluation* because you assess it while it is being formed.

Formative evaluation contrasts with *summative evaluation.* Summative evaluation assesses the effectiveness of a training program that is generally available, such as a classroom course that is listed in a course catalog and available for enrollment, or a workbook that learners can order and use now. Kirkpatrick's four levels of evaluation, which was introduced in chapter 1 and further discussed in chapter 4, is the framework for approaching summative evaluation.

The sole purpose of a formative evaluation described in this chapter is improving the draft training program to increase the likelihood that it will achieve its objectives when it becomes generally available. As a result, you conduct a formative evaluation while the training program is under development and use the findings to revise the training program before it becomes generally available to learners.

Specifically, the formative evaluation assesses these characteristics of the training program:

- *Clarity:* Learners should be able to comprehend content on the first explanation and follow exercises with no additional assistance, other than that provided in the instructions. Learners should not be slowed by inconsistencies in content or terminology, nor by grammatical errors or awkwardly presented content.
- *Accuracy:* The material should be current, correct, and complete.
- *Performance:* Printed pages should match those on the screen in word processors. Slides should appear on the projector as they do on the computer screen. Addresses of websites shown to class should be accurate and currently working. Hands-on exercises should work as intended.

The Three Basic Types of Formative Evaluation

To make sure your training program is clear, accurate, and performs properly, conduct these three types of formative evaluations: pilot tests, in which you run the training program for the first time with people who represent the intended learners; technical reviews, in which SMEs verify the accuracy of the content; and production reviews, in which editors assess the completeness and style of the content, and production specialists make sure that the printed and projected output matches your intentions.

Pilot Tests

A pilot test is one in which you take the training program for a trial run—that is, you deliver it for the first time to assess which parts work and which ones need improvement. When identifying parts of the training program that need further work, identify as specifically as possible what is not working and suggest possible improvements. You generally conduct a pilot test with the second draft of student materials and instructor's materials and with participants who have characteristics similar to those of the intended learners.

Because the draft training program has not been demonstrated yet to be effective and the results of the pilot test are only intended to assess whether the training program works, do not use the test results to assess the performance of learners. The pilot test might indi-

Basic Rule 38

A pilot test evaluates the training program, not the learners.

cate errors in teaching sequences, or tests or similar types of assessment activities, which, in turn, affect the performance of learners when performing the skills covered by the objectives.

To conduct a pilot test, follow this suggested procedure, adjusting it to the situation in your organization.

First, reserve a physical or virtual classroom for the pilot well in advance. For a physical classroom, make sure that it has the audiovisual and computer equipment needed (such as a projector for slides and computers for every learner for training programs with computer-based activities). Make sure that the classroom can be set up to meet your needs (for example, you might want learners to sit at tables so they can work in groups) and can accommodate the number of learners for the pilot. For a live virtual classroom, make sure that it can accommodate the desired number of learners (most virtual classrooms limit the number of people who can participate at one time). Also make sure that it has the technical capabilities needed to present the training program, such as the ability to display slides with animations (most virtual classroom software can show slides but some do not display animations), show the desktop of the instructor's computer, conduct polling questions, chat and speak with participants, and let participants enter the class using their smartphones and tablets, rather than just computers.

Second, recruit between eight and 15 learners to participate in the pilot. If you recruit fewer than eight, you might not receive a sufficiently broad perspective on the training program. If you recruit more than 15, however, you might not be able to debrief each learner. Learners recruited for the pilot should be supportive of the program or, at the very least, not openly hostile toward it. If you are a course developer and someone else will be teaching the training program when it becomes generally available, also recruit an instructor to teach the pilot so you can assess the effectiveness of the instructor's materials.

 Think About This

When preparing a self-study program, conduct a pilot in which you and your colleagues observe learners as they use the materials, called a *usability test*. When doing so, you might ask learners to speak aloud what they are thinking and feeling as they use the training program and record what they say. Because observations require full attention, you might only assess one person at a time, and because of the additional time needed to observe, you might only include five participants rather than eight to 12. Otherwise, the procedures for organizing a usability test are similar to the procedures for organizing a pilot class.

Third, send a reminder to all of the participants between two and five working days before the pilot of the training program is scheduled.

Fourth, prepare the materials. For face-to-face classroom pilots, print and copy student materials, including copies of slides, so you can distribute the materials when the training program starts. For live virtual classroom pilots, send the student materials before the program starts.

 Noted

To avoid the appearance of bias, ask a colleague to conduct the debriefing. If a colleague facilitates the discussion, you can record the comments and suggestions on your copies of materials.

Fifth, at the beginning of the pilot, remind learners that this is a test of the training program, not them. Reinforce that if learners do not understand something or feel that instructions could be clarified, learners should assume that the problem is with the training materials, not themselves. Ask learners to mark any issues on their copies of materials, describe their concerns, and offer suggestions (if they have any) for improvement. Also inform learners that you will pause to solicit their feedback at several points in the pilot.

Sixth, run the training program and, at appropriate intervals, pause and ask for feedback. This request for feedback is called a *debriefing*. Some instructors like to debrief a pilot after every unit because the comments on it are still fresh with learners. Other instructors like to debrief at the end of each day, to avoid interrupting the flow of the class. Choose an interval that feels comfortable to you.

Begin the debriefing by reminding learners again that the pilot is a test of the training program, not them. Then ask the learners some questions that solicit their feedback. For example: What material works well? What specific information or instructions were unclear? Do you have specific suggestions for improving them?

Seventh, at the end of the pilot, conduct an end-of-program debriefing that considers the entire training program, not just a single unit or day. Ask learners about their overall impressions of the program, and then ask them to identify parts of it that were effective and parts that need revision. Encourage learners to provide specific suggestions on ways to fix the problems they identified; the more specific their feedback, the better you can address their concerns. Conclude the debriefing by asking learners whether they plan to apply the skills in their jobs and, if they do not plan to do so, why, and what would help them to do so.

 Noted

If you have recruited an instructor to teach the pilot, also debrief the instructor. Find out which information the instructor felt was clear, and which information the instructor felt uncomfortable teaching and why she felt that way. Also ask the instructor to identify places in the instructor's materials where content could be strengthened.

Eighth, assess learners' performance on tests and assessment activities to make sure that questions and activities really address the objectives, that learners understand the instructions and questions, and that learners have really been taught the material so they have an opportunity to perform successfully on the assessments.

Last, after completing the pilot, review your notes. Categorize proposed comments as *A* (showstoppers—design and development should not continue before you address these issues), *B* (must change—although design and development of the program can continue, you must address these issues before making the program generally available), and *C* (nice to change—comments to address if time permits). Using these comments and their priorities as a guide, revise the training program, addressing category A and B issues before completing the program.

Technical Reviews

The second type of formative evaluation is a technical review. During a technical review, SMEs verify the accuracy of the content. Typically, technical reviews occur after completing each draft of a training program, except after the final draft.

Technical reviews are important because they ensure that learners receive complete, accurate, error-free information from the training program. Errors pose a serious legal liability. In regulated industries, such as the pharmaceutical industry, incorrect material could cause learners to perform their jobs incorrectly, which could create life-threatening situations (such as a doctor prescribing the wrong medicine).

The most common type of technical review is a reading review. One useful alternative is the walk-through. The following sections describe how to perform both.

Reading Reviews

During a reading review, designated people read through the draft of the training materials and assess the technical accuracy of the material. Accuracy is assessed from a number of perspectives. Technical experts focus on the completeness and accuracy of the materials. A marketing specialist assesses whether the training program reflects the marketing message for the product and the organization's brand. User experience specialists—people who assess the ease with which people can use products and services—assess whether users will be able to achieve the intended objectives with the training program.

Basic Rule 39

The best way to ensure that the content is technically accurate is by asking several SMEs to simultaneously review the training program.

To make sure that you receive the most helpful review comments, consider following this suggested procedure when conducting reading reviews.

First, leave enough time for reviews in the production schedule. Generally, leave at least one day of review for every 100 pages of review material. If you distribute review materials electronically, also leave a half day for the files to arrive. (Although many systems distribute files immediately, some don't.) If you distribute printed review materials, leave at least two days at either end of the review to make copies and an additional one to five business days for shipping. However you conduct reviews, inform reviewers of the dates for upcoming reviews so they can plan ahead and schedule time on their calendars. If reviewers have schedule conflicts, you can adjust the review schedule now to address them.

Second, a few days before distributing it, send reviewers a reminder that the review draft is coming.

Third, distribute the review draft with instructions explaining what reviewers should and need not do. Reviewers should comment on the accuracy of the content, the flow of the material, and ways to make the information clearer. Reviewers need not comment on layout, which is likely to change, or grammatical issues, which are usually addressed later in the process. Close the instructions by reminding reviewers of the date that you expect to receive comments.

If possible, double space review drafts and format text in 12-point Times New Roman or Courier type to signal that the material is in draft form.

Fourth, after receiving comments and acknowledging receipt to reviewers, go through the comments to determine which ones you intend to incorporate. (You do not have to incorporate all comments, though you need to explain why you chose to pass over a comment.) If you have questions about the comments (for example, if one comment contradicts a comment made by another reviewer), make notes, and then follow up with the reviewers or schedule a review meeting to discuss the questions. If you do not plan to incorporate a comment, briefly explain why.

Last, after you have incorporated the comments, send a follow-up note to reviewers describing the status of the comments. Depending on the culture of your organization, you might send one note that addresses all reviews, personalized notes to individual reviewers, or some combination.

Walk-Throughs

In some instances, a reading review does not elicit the depth of feedback needed to ensure that the training program is accurate. In such situations, consider conducting a series of walk-throughs.

In a walk-through, reviewers meet to read through the printed drafts of the course materials, going through each page and slide, one at a time. While doing so, reviewers comment on any parts that work well, parts that are inaccurate, and parts that need clarification or similar improvements. As reviewers raise one concern, participants in the walk-through determine as a group how to address it before proceeding with the review. If reviewers disagree, participants resolve the disagreement before proceeding.

Walk-throughs are especially useful for training programs on products and software for which the course designers and developers do not have access to prototypes. They are also useful for abstract processes, such as troubleshooting, for which no single correct procedure exists and for instances in which SMEs have a history of conducting inadequate reviews and the only way to get reviews from them is by forcing them to walk through the material in front of others.

When preparing for a walk-through, schedule a series of meetings: one for each unit of the training program, rather than a single meeting to address the entire program. Schedule two or three hours for each meeting. Also try to schedule the meetings on consecutive days for a period of one to two weeks, rather than stretching them out over several weeks. This ensures that the course material remains fresh in the reviewers' minds.

If you expect the review meetings to be challenging, also enlist a colleague who has no association with the project to facilitate them. Because someone else is facilitating the walk-throughs, you can focus your energies on clarifying the material and recording decisions. Should conflict arise, an external facilitator will take the lead in resolving it.

Production Reviews

The third type of formative evaluation is a production review, during which editors assess the completeness and style of the content, and production specialists make sure that the fully formatted output of the program, such as slides projected from the computer and printouts of student materials, appears as it was designed.

Basic Rule 40

Although heavily focused on details, production reviews are essential to the success of a training program because they ensure the clarity, consistency, and performance of the instructional materials.

Many course designers and developers dismiss production reviews as services that add little value because they focus mainly on such issues as capitalization, fonts, and page breaks. But a small typographical error can cause a significant change in meaning, and layout problems can confuse learners. Too many grammatical errors can detract from the credibility of a training program, as some learners reason, "If they can't get their spelling right, how can I be sure that they have the facts straight?" Taking production reviews seriously helps make sure that training programs maintain their accuracy and credibility.

Ideally, editors serve as the "first learner" of a training program. When given a chance to review all drafts of materials, editors can also play a substantive role, working closely with course designers and developers to fortify the structure of their courses, to identify and resolve unclear passages, and to enhance the presentation of information so that users can most easily comprehend it. This task is called *developmental* or *substantive editing*.

In many organizations, though, editors review a training program only once, just before it goes to final production. At that point, editors focus on grammar, spelling, punctuation, style, and other mechanical aspects of text—a task called *copyediting*. Copyediting also looks at the layout of slides, screens, and pages to ensure consistency of design across student and instructor materials, appropriate use of templates, correct and consistent use of headings, consistent style for charts and tables, proper placement of illustrations and graphics, clearly marked margins, and correct and consistent use of fonts, especially emphasis type such as boldface and italics.

In addition to copyediting, production reviews for self-study e-learning programs also involve verifying that the program runs as intended. Such reviews assess whether the programming works as planned (for example, if a student chooses an option, does the system display that option or something else)—a *functional test;* the effect of using the program while other programs are also running—a *system test;* and the number of students who can take the program at the same time—a *load test.*

Think About This

Because many training groups do not have editors on staff, course designers and developers review one another's programs. This is called *peer editing* because their peers (co-workers) perform the editing.

So if your training group does not provide access to editors, do not skip the editing step. The extra set of eyes of your peers usually finds glaring typographical and stylistic errors that you cannot find in your own work because you have such a close relationship with it.

If a peer is only available to review the training program once, schedule that review for the last draft, to ensure that the final product is as free of mechanical, stylistic, and visual errors as possible.

Revising the Training Program

Using the feedback received through each of the reviews as a guide, revise the draft of the training program. The following sections explore two issues that arise during revision: responding to feedback and addressing the revisions.

Responding to Feedback

One of the most challenging aspects of a course designer and developer's job is receiving comments on draft work. Some comments might be positive. But others might call for revisions, sometimes substantial revisions. And some comments can be so vague that you cannot understand the concern, much less determine how to improve the training program. Responding to comments with dignity and grace is one of the true tests of professionalism for any course designer and developer.

Consider the following suggestions when responding to feedback:

- Whenever possible, schedule comments to arrive on a Monday or Tuesday. By receiving comments on a Monday or Tuesday, you can immediately begin work on correcting them instead of worrying about them all weekend.
- Wait one business day before formally responding to any comments. The extra time gives you chance to plot a course of action. It also gives you an opportunity to calm down should any comment raise your blood pressure.
- Try to understand where reviewers are coming from. Some reviewers might make comments without thinking and are unintentionally abrupt. Others might write only part of what they are actually thinking, and you might be arriving at conclusions based on incomplete comments.
- Speak to the reviewer. Rather than avoid the situation, face it head on—and with an open mind. The resulting conversation is likely to be educational and enlightening.

Basic Rule 41

Assume that all feedback has some value. Make sure that you understand the underlying issue in feedback from each reviewer and how addressing the issue can strengthen the training program.

- When responding to vague or derogatory comments, ask the reviewer for clarification on the comment. When requesting clarification, explain as best as possible what you do not understand. By asking for clarification and avoiding a value judgment ("That comment is useless!"), you are likely to start a meaningful conversation.

These suggestions can help you open a dialogue without creating a confrontation and, in the process, forge stronger relationships with reviewers. Dialogues like the ones suggested here help course designers and developers find value in the comments and help reviewers better appreciate the work of course designers and developers. The dialogues become teachable moments for trainer and reviewer alike.

Noted

Not all feedback will be negative. Reviewers share positive feedback too, like "This activity effectively surfaces learners' prior knowledge," "What an amazingly clear definition," and an old favorite, "This is the best training program we've ever seen!"

Addressing the Revisions

Two types of changes arise from the revisions: within scope and outside of scope. Each requires a different approach, and the following sections tackle the two in detail.

Within-Scope Changes

Within-scope changes are ones that pertain to material that you agreed to cover in the design plans for the program as well as presentation approaches agreed on at that time. When incorporating within-scope changes, closely follow the essence of the suggested change. In some cases, this means incorporating the requested change verbatim. For example, if an attorney changes all of the instances of the word *can* to *may,* incorporate the change verbatim. The change is not a grammatical one; it is rooted in legal meaning. The word *can* makes an implied promise to consumers; the word *may* does not and, therefore, reduces the sponsor's potential liability in a lawsuit.

In other cases, adopt the essence of the change but alter the suggested wording, if any was provided. For example, a programmer might suggest adding a step to a procedure but writes the step in the third person and uses the passive voice. You can rewrite it in the second person and use the active voice, to be consistent with the rest of the procedure. Use your best judgment for determining when to follow a change verbatim and when to improvise.

Basic Rule 42

Always try to incorporate within-scope changes.

Within-scope changes also include changes that result from your new insights about the technical material. Designing and developing a training program is much like peeling away the layers of an onion. The further you progress in the process, the more you uncover. As you reach the later drafts of the process, you might experience "aha!" moments when your understanding deepens, and you want to incorporate that understanding into program materials. During the later drafts, the "aha!" moments usually pertain to small points and result in brief additional passages and sentences.

Within-scope changes might also enhance the quality of the presentation. As you go through the process of revision, you become increasingly sensitive to the finer aspects of instructional strategies. You become more aware of opportunities to make sections more parallel (structuring and presenting similar concepts in similar ways), strengthen the wording of certain passages, and present information graphically. If these changes only affect small passages (as long as a section) and as long as making these changes will not affect your original estimates of the budget and schedule, incorporate them.

For example, as you prepare the second draft, you might notice that a text passage could be replaced by a visual. You prepare the visual yourself using graphics software and distribute the draft on schedule. This is a within-scope change. Now, suppose that you are preparing the final draft and you see a similar opportunity to replace a text passage with a visual. But you need a graphic artist to prepare the visual and have already spent the funds allotted for graphics. This is an outside-of-scope change, which should be saved for a future edition of the training program.

Outside-of-Scope Changes

In the previous example, when a change to the graphics was deferred because the graphics budget had been exhausted, it's fair to wonder about the quality of the content and how a course designer and developer could have let an opportunity like this slip by before the final draft. But consider this: As you prepare a final draft, reviewers will not be reviewing the program again. To make sure that the sponsor and the reviewers agree with the change, you would need to schedule an additional review with them. That adds time to the process. And, because time is money, that increases the cost of the project.

Basic Rule 43

The decision of whether a change is appropriate ultimately is a business decision, one that takes into account the impact of the change on the budget and schedule of the project.

That cost pushes the project over your graphics budget, which means that you need even more funds to produce the unplanned visual. But the sponsor might feel that business needs do not warrant the additional expense. So although the change might improve the quality of the presentation, it comes at the expense of the quality of the management of the project.

In other words, this is an outside-of-scope change, one that either requires going outside of the material and instructional strategies in the design plans, or results in an avoidable deadline extension, cost increase, or both. Other examples of outside-of-scope changes include substantive changes to the technical information given to you by the SMEs that contradicts material provided earlier; substantive changes to the presentation of information, such as wholesale reorganizations of the program that were not discussed and approved during one of the review meetings; and substantial changes to several sections of the program.

These changes are outside of scope because they are not part of the original commitments. As a result, making the changes could delay the training program and, perhaps, increase its total cost. The manner in which you manage such changes could ultimately affect your relationship with the sponsor; in fact, management of changes is often the pivotal element of relationships between sponsors and course designers and developers. By carefully handling outside-of-scope changes, you can increase the likelihood that the relationship with the sponsor will remain intact and, at the same time, the changes will be handled responsibly. Table 9-1 shows some examples of how to manage the issues that arise from outside-of-scope changes.

Table 9-1. Managing Outside-of-Scope Changes

Who Initiated the Change?	How to Handle the Change
Sponsor	Inform the sponsor that the changes are outside the scope of the project and that, though you would be happy to make the change, you would need to renegotiate the schedule and budget. Although you might feel a moment of trepidation before renegotiating the schedule and budget, and although the sponsor might bristle when you raise the issue, do it anyway. In the long run, you stand a better chance of retaining the close relationship by asserting your needs now. Otherwise, you will be performing additional work on your own time and without compensation, and eventually resent it. If the sponsor agrees to adjust the schedule and budget and both of you commit to making the change, report the changes in the next project status document to inform all involved with the project.
You	Consider the full impact of these changes before pursuing them. Here are some issues to keep in mind: • The impact on the rest of the program, and the time needed to make changes. One change might have a cascading effect, such as a change in terminology that must be corrected in every unit of the program. • Whether the reviewers have adequate time to review the change. The later in the process (third or final draft), the less likely the reviewers have time to review the change. • The resources needed to produce the change. If you rely on others to implement the change, make sure that they are available to do so. Often, late in a project, graphic designers and other production staff have moved on to other projects. • The ultimate benefits to the learner and sponsor. If the ultimate benefit to either one of them is low, the change might not be appropriate. After considering these issues, if you still feel that the change is appropriate, request the sponsor's support before actually making the change.

Platinum, Silver, and Bronze Types of Projects

Because all training programs must be clear, accurate, and perform properly, formative evaluations occur for all three types of projects— platinum, silver, and bronze. The review process described in this chapter is for a platinum project (brand-new courses).

For silver and bronze projects, trainers might make adjustments. For a new silver or bronze program, trainers might forego the pilot test to contain costs. Instead, trainers might pay closer attention to the feedback from learners during the first few class sessions and adjust materials in response. Or, trainers might use peer reviews rather than professional editors when conducting the production reviews of silver and bronze projects.

For a revision to an existing project, trainers always conduct a technical review. But trainers usually call attention to changes directly on the draft so reviewers solely focus on the changed material. (Some trainers list the changes at the beginning of the draft but that usually does not help reviewers easily identify revised segments.) Because reviewers only focus on the changed material, many trainers avoid revisions to parts of a program not affected by the changes. Silver projects might undergo a production review, but bronze projects will likely rely on peer review.

Getting It Done

While designing and developing course materials, you conduct formative evaluation—that is, an assessment of the effectiveness of training programs while they are still under development—and address issues identified to increase the likelihood that, when published, programs achieve their intended objectives. Formative evaluation contrasts with summative evaluation, which assesses the extent to which training programs achieved their objectives after they are published—that is, become generally available.

Formative evaluation typically consists of three types of reviews: pilot tests, which take draft training programs for a trial run to assess the clarity and ease of use of the content and the logistics of the program; technical reviews, through which SMEs assess the accuracy of the content; and production reviews, which primarily consist of editing to identify inconsistencies, grammatical problems, and similar challenges and verifying that self-study online programs run as intended. Revise programs to reflect the feedback from these formative evaluations, while appropriately handling within-scope and out-of-scope changes.

Use Exercise 9-1 to guide you through the process of planning and coordinating the formative evaluation of a program you are currently developing.

Exercise 9-1. Planning the Formative Evaluation of a Training Program

Draft Level	Types of Evaluations	
First	Technical review	Name the reviewers and their roles: _____ _____ When review drafts will be distributed:_____ Date reminder notes to be sent: _____ When review drafts will be returned: _____
	Editorial review	Name the editor or peer reviewer: _____ When review draft will be distributed: _____ Date reminder notes to be sent: _____ When review drafts will be returned: _____
Second	Pilot test	When the class is scheduled: _____ Facility (physical classroom) or link (virtual classroom): _____ Special requirements for the classroom: _____ _____ Names of participants: _____ _____ Name the facilitator for comments (if using one): _____ Name the instructor (if someone other than you): _____ Date confirmation notes to be sent: _____ Date reminder notes to be sent: _____
	Technical review	Name the reviewers and their roles: _____ _____ When review drafts will be distributed: _____ Date reminder notes to be sent: _____ When review drafts will be returned: _____
	Editorial review	Name the editor or peer reviewer: _____ When review draft will be distributed: _____ Date reminder notes to be sent: _____ When review drafts will be returned: _____

(continued)

Exercise 9-1. Planning the Formative Evaluation of a Training Program (continued)

Draft Level	Types of Evaluations	
Third	Technical Review	Name the reviewers and their roles: _____ _____ When review drafts will be distributed: _____ Date reminder notes to be sent: _____ When review drafts will be returned: _____
	Editorial review	Name the editor or peer reviewer: _____ When review draft will be distributed: _____ Date reminder notes to be sent: _____ When review drafts will be returned: _____
Final	Editorial review	Name the editor or peer reviewer: _____ When review draft will be distributed: _____ Date reminder notes to be sent: _____ When review drafts will be returned: _____
	Production review	Name of the person conducting the functional test: _____ Name of the person conducting the system test:_____ Name of the person conducting the load test: _____

10

The Basics of Administering Training Programs

 What's Inside This Chapter

This chapter introduces the key activities in the implementation of training programs. Specifically, this chapter addresses the basics of:

- Administering training programs, including classroom coordination, enrollment, and follow-up
- Marketing training programs, such as the "must have" marketing information and "must consider" issues of scheduling (as it relates to marketing a program)
- Supporting training programs, including providing services to learners, maintaining the technical content, and managing the summative evaluation of the program
- Closing the design and development project.

An exercise at the end of this chapter helps you plan for administering, marketing, and supporting a training program on which you are working.

As a course designer and developer, you spend the bulk of your time and energy designing and developing a training program. But the success of your efforts depends on activities that happen after the training program becomes generally available—administering, marketing, and supporting the program. These activities create the foundation of the learning experience, and shape learners' perceptions of the program. Or put more directly: classrooms with poor air circulation and cold coffee, and incorrect links to a virtual classrooms influence learner perceptions of training programs as much as the learning experiences that course designers and developers carefully crafted.

 Basic Rule 44

The success of a training program depends on the administration, marketing, and support of it. But these activities can be challenging because other people often handle them. Planning for them during design and development can go a long way to ensuring that the training program achieves its goals.

As a result, although course designers and developers often are not responsible for administering, marketing, and supporting the programs they develop, planning for these activities during design and development and overseeing them when the programs go into general use can help ensure that the programs have the intended impact. This chapter provides an overview of these implementation activities and ends with a discussion of how to properly close a project.

Administering Training Programs

Administration, the first activity in implementation, refers to the activities involved in running physical and virtual classroom programs and distributing self-study programs—more specifically, scheduling programs, enrolling learners, preparing for programs, closing programs, and providing follow-up reports.

 Basic Rule 45

To make sure that your training program runs as planned, pay attention to the scheduling, enrollment processes, and setup of the classroom (physical or virtual), even if you do not plan to personally teach the program.

Scheduling Training Programs

One of the key factors in the success of a training program is scheduling it properly. Scheduling it right might mean programs exceed enrollment expectations, while ineffective scheduling might mean programs that few learners take.

For live programs, scheduling involves reserving the physical or virtual classroom space (and other facilities, if needed) and arranging for an instructor to teach the class session.

For self-study programs, courses are usually available whenever learners want to take them. In some organizations, however, learners take self-study programs in a learning center where they study in a quiet location that offers easy access to equipment, books, tutors, and other resources needed. Some organizations try to schedule learners to take self-study programs during slower periods in the work day (called *downtime* or *valleys*). Other organizations encourage workers in the field (such as inspectors and marketing representatives) to take programs while in transit between locations. And others encourage workers to take some self-study programs that are not directly applicable to their current jobs outside of work hours.

 **Noted**

As the course designer and developer, your primary interest in scheduling is making sure that your program is scheduled at optimum times and that the administrators have reserved the classrooms best suited to the program. For example, if your physical classroom program requires that learners have access to computers, you'll want to make sure that your program is scheduled in a computer lab.

Or you might have designed a virtual program that includes two-way video between instructor and students. Because this program needs a lot of bandwidth, the ideal scheduling is during shoulder periods of the day—before 10 a.m. or after 3:30 p.m.—to minimize the likelihood of network problems during the class session.

Consider these additional issues that affect scheduling:

- If you are scheduling a new program that each intended learner must take, schedule as many class sessions as possible to give learners options that fit their schedules. After completing the training of the initial group of learners, schedule classes on a regular, predictable schedule, such as the first week of every quarter, so people in the organization can plan around it.
- Avoid scheduling classes near public holidays. Generally, programs scheduled the same weeks as national holidays tend to draw poorly. Even when attendance is required and

learners show up, their minds might be on vacation. Also avoid scheduling classes on religious and cultural holidays, even if they affect a relatively small number of learners in your organization. Scheduling on these dates creates an unnecessary dilemma for some learners and may be interpreted as insensitive.

- For classes scheduled in the evening, avoid Friday evenings, which is considered by many as part of the weekend. Even if learners are attending a program for professional development, they generally prefer to do so on weeknights.
- For live programs that attract learners from many geographic locations, schedule classes where your learners are, in a location convenient for a majority.

Enrolling Learners and Confirming Their Registration

During enrollment, learners reserve seats in a live training program or start a self-study one. In many organizations, learners enroll in programs through a learning management system. In others, an administrator (a member of the training staff other than the course designer and developer) handles enrollment-related tasks.

After learners enroll in a live program, the learning management system sends a confirmation to the learner and, just before class starts (up to a week in advance), a reminder that learners are scheduled to attend. The confirmation and reminder messages state the name of the program, program number (if the organization uses them), date and time of the program, name of the instructor, reminders about charges (if any), and name of an administrator to contact with questions. For programs held in a face-to-face classroom, the confirmation letter provides the location, directions, and, if needed, travel information, including names of nearby hotels. For programs held in a virtual classroom, the confirmation letter provides the web address of the virtual classroom, as well as instructions for connecting to the classroom, including usernames and passwords. For a self-study program, the learning management system automatically generates a note that tells students how to access the materials and begin learning.

Figure 10-1 is an example of a confirmation letter for a virtual class. A reminder letter is just a variation on the confirmation letter.

Figure 10-1. Example of an Enrollment Confirmation Letter

Dear John:

This is a note to confirm your enrollment in the Virtual Sales School for New Marketing Representatives (course SS 100).

The course is scheduled:

Monday, November 17, through Friday, November 21
9:30 a.m. to 12:00 p.m. (EST)
Instructor: Steven Ip

The class is scheduled as a webinar. You attend class by connecting to a virtual classroom. To do so:

1. At least two days before class, make sure that you have:
   • A reliable Internet connection
   • A device that can connect to the Internet
   • Sound capability (so you can hear the instructor)
   • Typing capability (so you can interact with the instructor)

2. At least one day before class, visit this link to download the student materials: http://virtualclass. companyname.com/salesschool/studentmaterials.

3. Between 15 and 30 minutes before the scheduled start time of the course, connect to the classroom:

   a. Visit: http://virtualclass.companyname.com/salesschool.
   b. When the sign-in screen appears, provide the following information:
      Username: StudentJohn
      Password: JohnStudent2

   c. The system will download the virtual classroom software. This takes one to four minutes, depending on your Internet connection.
   d. When the download completes, the system displays the virtual classroom.
   e. At that time, the class instructor will prompt you to practice using the interactive components of the virtual classroom so you can fully participate.

Your department has been charged $495.00 for this class. If you cannot attend, please let us know two weeks in advance or your department will be charged. If you must cancel with fewer than two weeks' notice, your department will still be charged for the class, but may send an alternate in your place or reserve a space for you in a later class.

If you have questions about this course, please contact me at extension 4599 or trainingadmin@companyname.com.

Thank you for your enrollment. We look forward to seeing you in class.

Best regards,

Lucy Hyatt
Training Administrator

Most organizations have documented processes for handling class enrollments, including standardized enrollment and confirmation letters. As the course designer and developer, you should ensure that enrollment is easy. The easier the enrollment process, the more likely learners are to register for the program. Easy enrollment involves clear instructions (so that prospective learners know exactly what they need to do to enroll and what information they need to provide when doing so), appropriate documentation (any information required to accurately identify the learner and get enrollment and payment information, but not so much that the learner perceives the requests as cumbersome or intrusive), quick processing of the enrollment, and courteous handling of registration. Many organizations turn to learning management systems to automate the process.

You should also ensure that learners have the prerequisite knowledge when enrolling in programs. If learners do not, they will likely flounder. Many learning management systems can automatically verify whether learners have completed prerequisite programs before letting them enroll. If an administrator handles enrollment in your organization, you need to make sure that he checks for prerequisites.

Also make sure that learners receive all preclass announcements, such as work that they should complete before class (called *prework*) and a list of equipment they might need to bring to class.

These issues also apply to enrollment in self-study programs. The primary difference is that learners usually can begin self-study programs immediately after enrolling in them.

Preparing for Training Programs

Preparation is an activity in which the administrator makes sure that all of the resources are available for a class session. Whether it's for face-to-face or virtual training programs, preparing the setup properly can make the difference between enjoyable and unpleasant learning experiences, which can, in turn, influence whether the programs achieve their goals.

Face-to-Face Training Programs

To prepare for a class session of a face-to-face training program, you or the administrator should make sure that all the needed resources are available. For face-to-face programs, resources typically include:

- general supplies, such as markers for the whiteboards, paper for flip charts, name tags for learners (some organizations preprint them, others provide blank name tags for learners to fill out), and blank pads and pens

- any appropriate general information about the facility (emergency numbers, locations of restrooms, information about lunch facilities, and so forth)
- copies of the learner's materials, which usually consist of the student guide and other needed supplies. For example, learners in an equipment maintenance course might receive a screwdriver so that they could remove the external casing of the equipment
- materials for exercises. For computer-based exercises, make sure that all software and files have been installed, that passwords are set for each student and the instructor, and that each computer works. For other exercises, make sure that any special materials not already mentioned are available
- room setup instructions, which specify the arrangement of tables. Figure 10-2 shows the choices available for room arrangements
- for programs with audiovisual materials, make sure the classroom has a slide or overhead projector, as well as video, CD, or DVD players, speakers, monitors, and microphones
- refreshments (if provided, as many organizations do)
- postclass evaluation forms (especially if the name of the program and instructor and date of the class session are preprinted on the form).

Because improper preparations for physical classrooms can lead to an unpleasant class experience, make sure to provide a setup list that specifies the general supplies needed; audiovisual requirements; and classroom setup. Also provide a master copy of the learners' materials for copying and binding, as well as any unique instructions that administrators must consider as they copy and bind the materials (as discussed in chapters 7 and 8).

Preparation for Virtual Training Programs

Although virtual training programs require no physical setup, they do require technical setup. Several preparations are required.

First, someone must upload slides and other documents used in the class to the virtual classroom and make sure that they appear as designed.

Figure 10-2. Typical Setups for Physical Classrooms

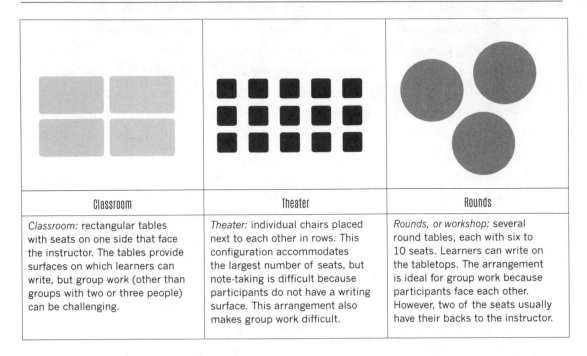

Classroom	Theater	Rounds
Classroom: rectangular tables with seats on one side that face the instructor. The tables provide surfaces on which learners can write, but group work (other than groups with two or three people) can be challenging.	*Theater:* individual chairs placed next to each other in rows. This configuration accommodates the largest number of seats, but note-taking is difficult because participants do not have a writing surface. This arrangement also makes group work difficult.	*Rounds, or workshop:* several round tables, each with six to 10 seats. Learners can write on the tabletops. The arrangement is ideal for group work because participants face each other. However, two of the seats usually have their backs to the instructor.

Second, someone must program all of the polling questions so that they operate as intended. Someone must create special slides with the polling questions and options, and make sure that they work as intended, too.

Third, someone must arrange the layout of the screen to meet the preferences of the instructor.

Most of all, instructors must practice using the technology of the virtual classroom as well as practice with all of the interactive elements that will be used in class to make sure that the instructor is comfortable facilitating these interactions. Even experienced online instructors require practice when using a particular virtual classroom application for the first time because, like different car manufacturers vary the controls in a car, different publishers of virtual classroom software vary the controls for virtual classrooms.

Some organizations expect instructors to manage classrooms without assistance. In such instances, instructors handle most of this preparation on their own but must receive general training on the administration and operation of a virtual classroom before using the classroom the first time. Other organizations make a webcasting producer available, who often sets up the classroom. Regardless of the person doing it, setup usually occurs between one and five business days before the scheduled class. Preparing a setup list for a virtual class, which indicates the files to upload, the interactions to pre-program, and other instructions, organizes the setup process and ensures that it operates as efficiently as possible.

Closing Training Programs

Closing a training program involves making sure that learners receive credit for participation and that the physical or virtual classroom is returned to its original state. Specifically, closing a program involves:

- giving credit to those learners who complete the program requirements. In some instances, anyone who attends the program receives credit for participation. In other instances, learners must have met additional requirements, such as passing a posttest
- providing certificates to learners who complete the program (optional, but a popular means of recognizing learners for completing training programs)
- for a physical classroom, cleaning it and returning any equipment borrowed from other locations
- for a virtual classroom, saving and then deleting any class chats and documents created just for the class session (such as drawings made during class on a virtual whiteboard)
- for all types of classes, collecting evaluations. Most organizations conduct satisfaction (Level 1) evaluations. Some do so at the end of a class; others send a note to participants with a link to the evaluation within one to three business days of the completion of the program. Other organizations also evaluate learning (Level 2). They typically administer the test or learning activity at the end of the program, but might not be able to report results right away.

As an instructor, your primary concern is making sure that the learners who complete requirements receive credit for completing the training program, encouraging learners to complete the evaluation, and, in those instances in which learners take a test or similar evaluation of learning, providing them with their score—that is, feedback on their performance.

Providing Follow-Up Reports

In many organizations, administrators perform follow-up activities after a class ends, such as providing a summary of class evaluations, providing a summary of learner performance on tests and similar assessments of learning (when offered), providing a report of the class completions, and sending a postclass follow-up (usually a Level 3 evaluation) and compiling and reporting the responses.

Course designers and developers take a special interest in these reports because they usually provide information about the number of people who attended a class, their opinions of it, and the material that stuck after training. Some administrators automatically distribute this information, but you might need to request that they share the reports with you.

Marketing Training Programs

Marketing, the second activity in implementation, involves planning announcements and promotions for new training programs. These announcements and promotions are essential to the success of training programs because they need active promotion if people are to enroll in them.

The following sections describe marketing issues that affect course designers and developers: the must-have materials, additional promotional materials, and the promotional plan.

 **Noted**

In most organizations, the course designer and developers are responsible for marketing the training program, even if they do not have general marketing responsibilities (much less training in how to market a program).

Must-Have Marketing Materials

To promote a new training program, you first prepare marketing materials for it. As banks require a tangible guarantee called collateral before making most loans, marketing efforts require some tangible information called *marketing collateral* before a new program can be announced and promoted. Collateral remains available throughout the life of the program. For a training program, this marketing collateral is the program description (Figure 10-3).

Figure 10-3. Program Description

Managing Technical Communication Groups
Length: 2 days
Format: Classroom
About this program: Effectively managing a technical communication group involves a unique set of skills: clearly communicating expectations regarding a job, effectively evaluating performance, establishing a vision for your group, making a business case for proposed projects, and selling the services of your group. This certificate program helps you develop these skills.

This program develops these skills through a combination of discovery exercises (which leverage your existing knowledge), formal presentations (which describe the "must-knows"), and action planning segments, which give you a chance to consider how you'll apply what you learned back on the job.

You'll learn how to:
- manage the performance planning and evaluation process, in which you plan for and communicate your expectations regarding specific jobs and evaluate the extent to which workers have achieved them
- motivate your workers
- develop a strategic plan for your group
- prepare a business case for proposed projects
- market services to skeptical internal customers (or sponsors).

Note: Although this certificate program addresses many aspects of management, it does not specifically address project management. A list of relevant readings will be provided for your information should you choose to explore this topic on your own.

Who should attend: Managers and supervisors of technical communication groups with one year or less of experience in their management roles; senior technical communicators who are planning to move into management within the next year.

Promotional Material

The second part of the marketing a training program involves preparing promotional material for it. Promotional material raises awareness of a program in the short run and is only intended to have a shelf life of four to 12 weeks.

 Basic Rule 46

Every training program must have a program description for marketing purposes. A description typically contains (1) the program title; (2) length (the number of hours or days); (3) 50–75-word description that motivates readers to take the program while accurately describing it; (4) objectives; (5) audience (descriptive information about intended learners); and (6) any prerequisites (typically stated as program titles, but more helpful if the program titles are preceded by naming the skills learners should master before starting the program).

Some traditional forms of promotional material include flyers about the program, posters, and banner ads on corporate websites (including intranet sites), which catch the eye quickly. Also try using email to announce or promote the training program, usually sent to graduates of previous programs and people who fit the demographic profile of the intended learners.

A popular form of promotional material is social media. For training groups promoting programs within their organizations, consider using a corporate social media system (like Yammer) or online announcement system over the organization's intranet. For training groups promoting programs outside of their organizations, consider using LinkedIn, Twitter, Facebook, and other social media.

To ensure that the message has the strongest impact on social media, use every available channel—most prospective learners only follow one or two services. When promoting a program, keep the announcements brief, focusing on the availability of the program and its scheduled dates (or indicate that the program is self-study). Include a link to the program description and other in-depth material about the program in the announcement to provide further information and enrollment instructions. And on each social media platform, share three variations of the message over a 24-hour period to increase the likelihood that the intended audience will see it.

More off-the-wall promotions include fortune cookies with custom-printed fortunes that recommend your training program, cakes decorated with a message about your training program, and other edible items (perhaps distributed in the employee cafeteria or break room).

Promotional Plan

After identifying the materials needed to promote the training program, prepare a plan for how you will use them and when, so you make the most effective use of your limited marketing resources. Here is a suggested timeline:

- Before the training program is available, prepare marketing collateral and make sure that it is ready for the day of announcement. Also prepare some promotional material that will raise awareness of the program. Finally, generate good advance support for the program, such as piloting the program with a group beforehand. Capitalize on the experiences of pilot participants to generate positive word of mouth, which should inspire others to consider the training program.
- A month to six weeks after the training program becomes available, prepare another wave of promotional material to maintain the awareness of the training program following its initial launch.

- For classroom programs (physical or virtual), promote the availability 10–12 weeks before each class session.
- For self-study programs, promote the availability on an ongoing basis (quarterly or semiannually).
- When enrollment starts to slow down, plan another round of promotional material to rebuild awareness of the training program. Ongoing publication of a catalog also helps to maintain awareness. If enrollment fails to improve, consider a major revision to the program or withdrawing it, as demand no longer exists for the current version of the program.

Budget time in your schedule to perform these activities. Organizations that market products and services externally devote as much as 20 percent of their resources to marketing. Although that is not feasible when marketing internally, failing to devote more than an hour or two to promotion could doom the training program to low usage and poor evaluation results.

 Noted

When should you send marketing announcements about individual class sessions for physical and virtual training programs?

Send first announcements of class sessions 10–12 weeks before they are scheduled—no sooner, no later. Training consultant Don Schroello conducted research that found that when prospective learners received first announcements more than 12 weeks before class, they filed the note away to come back to later but rarely did, and that when they received first announcements fewer than 10 weeks before a class—even in the age of the Internet and instant communication—prospective learners might have already made plans during the class dates.

As an incentive to encourage prospective students to enroll early—and avoid last minute enrollments—offer early registration discounts, late registration penalties, and similar incentives.

Follow-up announcements sent between eight and nine weeks before the class session and, again, four and five weeks before support the marketing effort.

Supporting Training Programs

Support, the third activity in implementation, involves providing services to learners, maintaining the content, and managing evaluations. In some cases, the course designer and developer is responsible for support. In other cases, a training administrator handles these tasks. Regardless, when not providing the support personally, the course designer and developer still needs to monitor the support provided by others because that support directly reflects on the course designer and developer anyway.

Providing Support to Learners

Despite your best attempts to explain content clearly, some learners might not understand it. Other learners might seek enrichment or individual attention not available in the classroom. In these and similar instances, organizations provide services to learners primarily through tutoring and enrichment.

Basic Rule 47

The support that you provide to learners leaves a lasting impression about the entire learning experience.

Tutoring

Tutoring provides learners with one-to-one assistance to help them master content they have difficulty comprehending. Some learners receive tutoring face-to-face, either through office hours (a regularly scheduled time and place where learners can visit to receive tutoring) or a scheduled appointment. More commonly, learners receive e-tutoring, or assistance through some form of mediated communication, such as email, telephone, or virtual office hours (instant messaging or video chat by Skype, FaceTime, or Google Hangouts).

Regardless of how your organization provides it, promote the availability of tutoring before and during class. Before class, many learners and their managers might perceive tutoring as a value-added service or see it as an incentive for enrolling. During class, learners might realize they need it.

One challenge in providing tutoring is setting clear expectations. For example, how soon should learners expect a response after requesting tutoring assistance? Many learners expect immediate responses, but that is not always feasible. Similarly, how long after the program is completed can learners receive tutoring services? Some providers offer tutoring for up to six months after a class.

If someone other than you will provide tutoring services, that person must become familiar with the content of the program before its launch, and you should provide the tutor with a list of anticipated questions and suggested responses.

No matter who tutors, anticipate how much staff time will be needed for tutorial support and schedule it. Otherwise, questions will seem like interruptions, and learners might be treated with less than the consideration they deserve. The actual time to schedule varies, depending on how many learners take the training program and whether your organization only provides tutoring during the class or for a period of time afterward. At first, you might set aside the same amount of time that a typical college professor leaves for office hours: between two and four hours a week. As the program progresses, monitor the actual time spent to determine how much time to allot to tutoring in the future.

Enrichment

Enrichment allows learners to enhance their experience with the instructional material through continuing study of the subject. The study might involve going further in depth or exploring specialized applications. Typically, enrichment consists of additional readings on a topic, such as magazine and news articles, academic research, and informative websites; links to organizations and publications that regularly publish material online about the subject; and links to online discussions—such as LinkedIn discussion groups and Facebook pages—with ongoing conversations about the topic.

Course designers and developers often provide enrichment online. For a live program, course designers and developers offer web-based materials through the learning management system or create a separate website, access to which is limited to former students of the program. For self-study programs, course designers and developers often include an optional enrichment unit and let students retain access to the program after completion to use these materials.

The main challenge of providing enrichment resources for course designers and developers is setting aside the time to prepare and maintain them.

Maintaining the Content

Maintenance of the content means periodically checking material in the program to make sure that it remains accurate and clear. Accuracy poses an ongoing challenge because some content goes out of date fairly quickly. For example, product information, policies, procedures, regulations, laws, and organizational structures change frequently, so the training programs that mention them must be updated in turn.

Most organizations provide advance notice of such changes, which allows you to plan for them. For example, if you develop a training program about a new medical device and you know that new models or enhancements will be made available six to nine months later, you can schedule the necessary updates to the program.

Generally, revisions fall into three categories:
- minor, which involves changes to specific passages (and usually just a word or sentence here and there), an occasional paragraph, and perhaps a new or changed illustration in the slides or supplemental materials
- moderate, which involves the addition of new sections, as well as changes to specific passages and graphics
- major, which involves a complete overhaul of the program.

Determine the extent of the revisions to estimate the resources needed to make them. Between revisions, keep a file of changes suggested by learners and others who use the program to make the next time you update the program.

Managing the Evaluation of the Program

As part of the early phases of design, you developed the plan for conducting the summative evaluation of the program. You prepared drafts of surveys to assess satisfaction, tests and other activities to assess learning, and follow-up assessments to assess transfer before you even decided how to format and present the instructional materials.

As you prepare for the launch and maintain the program, also plan to administer the summative evaluations, and compile and report the results of these evaluations, which are regularly conducted when the program goes into general use. Specifically, consider:
- Updating the evaluation instruments. Because you wrote the evaluations before developing the content and might have made adjustments to the objectives of the training program as you designed and developed that program, make sure that evaluations reflect those changes if you have not already done so during the later activities in development.
- Planning how to administer the evaluations. Consider how you will solicit feedback on satisfaction. Will you ask every student to complete a form before they leave the classroom, or will you use follow-up emails and phone calls (especially helpful with self-study programs, as learners are less likely to respond to satisfaction surveys)? Consider, too, how you will assess learning. Will you administer a formally proctored test, complete with someone in the room to prevent cheating? If so, who will serve as proctor? To whom will you report results? How will you track follow-up surveys that provide evidence of long-term changes in behavior resulting from the learning? How

will you contact learners about the follow-up surveys: by email, phone, or some other method? Whom else will you survey to assess whether learners are applying the content taught in the training program on the job?

- Reporting the results. Specifically, consider who receives results: Members of the learning team? The sponsor for whom you developed the training program? Next consider what format the reports will take. At the least, answer these questions. At the most, determine whether different groups receive different reports. Prepare prototypes of each evaluation report you plan to provide with "dummy" data and show the prototypes to stakeholders to see whether the reports would provide them with useful data. If not, make adjustments so the reports are useful to stakeholders.

Closing a Design and Development Project

Complete a course design and development project by formally closing it. Closing the project involves conducting a postmortem and preparing a project history file.

Basic Rule 48

Provide complete records of a training project—about the experience of developing it (through a postmortem) and the history of its progress (through a project history course)—so other course designers and developers can learn from the experience.

Conducting a Postmortem

A postmortem is a process that occurs after a project is complete and in which the development team identifies the lessons from the experience: the activities and decisions that worked well, those that didn't, and the deeper insights gained that can be carried into future projects. One of the most effective methods of identifying these lessons is a special meeting of the project team, called a *postmortem meeting*.

A postmortem meeting occurs after the program has been made generally available. It includes all members of the project team: SMEs, graphic designers, sponsors, your manager, and, of course, you. Its purpose is to identify what went well and what should be repeated on future projects, and what did not go well and how to avoid these situations on future projects.

Start the meeting by asking the team to share what went right; this establishes a productive tone for the meeting. Starting with the positive also helps end the project on a high note because, by the time a project wraps, team members are often focused on what went wrong. Only after discussing what went right should the discussion focus on things to improve in future projects. And to the extent possible, focus not only on identifying issues that need to be handled differently in the future, but also on offering suggestions for how to handle these issues. That keeps the focus of the postmortem on learning from the experience, not just on blaming team members.

Further, create a productive environment by providing each team member with an opportunity to speak. For example, when you ask "What went right?" and "What do we need to improve on future projects?" go around the room and ask each person to provide at least one suggestion, rather than merely asking for volunteers to share their thoughts—and dominate the conversation.

Also avoid passing judgment on comments. As a result of their role or because of their personalities, different team members have different perceptions about the project. Some might have had a positive experience, and others not. Only by hearing how each team member perceived the project can the entire development team better understand the just-completed project.

 **Noted**

> The postmortem should provide time for everyone on the development team to thank one another for their contributions. Often during the course of a project, team members become so comfortable working with one another that they forget to thank others for their contributions or acknowledge exceptional work. As a result, team members might not realize that their colleagues appreciate these contributions. The postmortem thus allows team members to offer one another such recognition.

Here are some tips for conducting a postmortem:

- Send a meeting notice to team members at least two weeks in advance. Invite all team members to participate, including representatives from the sponsoring organization.
- Prepare and distribute an agenda before the meeting. A typical postmortem is 60 minutes, and should be no longer than 90 minutes. The agenda should set aside time for discussing what went well, identifying what needs to be improved for future projects, and offering acknowledgments and thanks to the team members.

- Identify a recorder to keep the minutes and distribute them after the meeting.
- Close the postmortem with some sort of celebration. For example, you could provide a cake that says "Congratulations" or a small gift for each team member.
- Publish the minutes of the postmortem, ideally within two business days.
- For those suggestions that require changes to your organization's policies and procedures, provide a follow-up memo to team members within a month of the meeting to tell them whether the policy and procedures will be changed.

Postmortems provide valuable closure to projects, letting participants emotionally separate from one project so they can move onto the next, while ending on a positive note. Therefore, postmortem meetings are beneficial regardless of whether team members will work together on their next projects.

Preparing a Project History File

A project history file is a repository of all key information about the development of a training program. Although each organization requests different information for a project history file, some common elements include:

- project proposal
- report of the needs analysis
- design plans
- prototypes
- copies of each draft
- feedback from any pilot tests
- copies of comments submitted for each plan and draft
- copies of the planned and actual budgets and schedules
- at least two hard copies and backup electronic copies of all finished program materials and accompanying materials
- lists of all activities used in programs (especially if your organization reuses activities across programs, so developers of future programs can determine whether their learners have already experienced these activities)
- minutes of the postmortem meeting and other lessons learned
- names of contacts.

This information can be can be used in a number of different ways. One is that records of the time and cost of each completed activity can be used as tools to estimate the schedules and budgets of future projects. The more you base future estimates on past performance, the more accurate they are likely to become.

Similarly, records of proposals and needs analyses can be used as input to future projects, too. They can be reused to reduce the time needed to prepare similar materials. Or they can serve as one of many sources of input for a future project.

Design plans can be reused or serve as a framework for building designs of new programs (much like architects base designs for future buildings on previous ones). The programming code for online courses or computer-based activities can be adapted for future projects, too. And lessons learned can be used to improve the overall management of a project.

Save the project history file in a secure place. Keep an electronic copy on a server accessible to all members of the training group, as well as additional backups should anything happen to the copy on the server. In addition, if your company has an offsite archive, also store both the online and printed versions of the history file there.

Platinum, Silver, and Bronze Types of Projects

This chapter described the implementation phase of a platinum project. The same implementation issues also arise during silver and bronze projects, but the implementation decisions might differ.

Consider these differences for silver and bronze projects when administration is handled by a person rather than a learning management system. Enrollment processes generally involve fewer notifications (perhaps just a confirmation) and they usually occur more slowly than the system automatically handling them. Marketing efforts might be limited to a program description in a catalog and a single announcement of the availability of a program. Support for tutoring or enrichment might not even be available. Maintenance is likely to occur less frequently, especially with bronze projects, because the content is not as critical to the organization. To close a project, funds might not be available for a formal celebration.

In addition, when a silver or bronze project is a revision to an existing training program, the primary focus of the implementation phase involves updates to the existing support. For example, the learning management system might automatically send confirmation letters that mention the former name of the program. So when planning for implementation, make sure to update the letters and other materials. Furthermore, if you notice that earlier plans overlooked something, address it when planning for implementation of the revision and indicate that the issue was overlooked before. For example, an earlier implementation plan might not have planned for maintenance of the content. Make sure that the new implementation plan addresses any overlooked aspects.

Getting It Done

After completing the design and development of a training program, your responsibilities continue. By paying attention to administration, marketing, and support, you can make sure that the program works as well in practice as you had hoped it would when designing it. Administration involves scheduling, enrollment, and classroom coordination. Marketing involves preparing marketing collateral, related promotional material, and a promotional plan for using them. Support involves providing services to learners, scheduling maintenance to the content, and managing the evaluation of the program. Afterward, close the project by holding a postmortem meeting and preparing a project history file.

Use Exercise 10-1 to guide you through the process of administering, marketing, and supporting a training program.

Exercise 10-1. Administering, Marketing, and Supporting Training Programs

Preparing for class sessions	❑ General supplies
	❑ Room setup
	❑ Special materials for exercises
	❑ Audiovisual equipment (face-to-face only)
	❑ Learners' materials
	  __ Face-to-face classroom program: Bring printed copies or electronically distribute them in advance
	  __ Virtual classroom programs: How will copies be distributed to learners?
	❑ Closing a class
	  __ Processing completions
	  __ Providing completion certificates
	  __ Physical classroom programs: Returning the classroom to the condition in which it was before the program
	  __ Virtual classroom programs: Saving and then removing chats and other traces of this particular class session
	  __ Processing evaluations
	❑ Providing follow-up reports on attendance and evaluation

(continued)

Exercise 10-1. Administering, Marketing, and Supporting Training Programs (continued)

Distributing self-study materials	Materials needed by learners (such as workbooks)	How will you distribute them to learners?
Marketing the program	☐ Prepare a program description ☐ Prepare social media announcements ☐ Prepare special promotions, like flyers and edible promotions ☐ Prepare a promotional plan that promotes the program at these times: __ Upon announcement __ Within a month or so of announcement __ Ongoing marketing __ When enrollment slows down	
Scheduling the class sessions	☐ Announce class session 10–12 weeks in advance ☐ Avoid high vacation times ☐ Avoid religious and other holidays	
Providing support to learners	☐ Tutoring How will you provide it? _____ ☐ Enrichment How will you provide it? _____	
Maintaining the program	List planned updates to the program material: ☐ In three months. Type of revision: __ Minor __ Moderate __ Major ☐ Changes anticipated: _____ ☐ In six months. Type of revision: __ Minor __ Moderate __ Major ☐ Changes anticipated: _____ ☐ In nine months. Type of revision: __ Minor __ Moderate __ Major ☐ Changes anticipated: _____ ☐ In 12 months. Type of revision: __ Minor __ Moderate __ Major ☐ Changes anticipated: _____	
Closing a project	☐ Conduct a postmortem ☐ Prepare a project history file with two copies of these: __ Project proposal __ Report of the needs analysis __ Design plans __ Prototypes __ Copies of each draft __ Feedback from any tests of pilot tests __ Copies of comments submitted for each plan and draft __ Copies of the planned and actual budgets and schedules	

This chapter concludes the discussion of how to design and develop training programs. This book has taken you through all the ADDIE activities. After defining some background principles in chapter 1 and offering guidance for starting a project in chapter 2, this book walked you through analysis (chapters 3 and 4), design (chapters 5 and 6), development (chapters 7, 8, and 9), and implementation and evaluation (chapter 10).

References

Alred, G.J., C.T. Brusaw, and W.E. Oliu. 2000. *Handbook of Technical Writing.* 6th ed. New York: St. Martin's Press.

Arthur, W., W. Bennett, P.S. Edens, and S.T. Bell. 2003. "Effectiveness of Training in Organizations: A Meta-Analysis of Design and Evaluation Features." *Journal of Applied Psychology* 88(2): 234-245.

Carliner, S. 2002. *Designing E-Learning.* Alexandria, VA: ASTD Press.

Chapman, B. 2010. "How Long Does It Take to Create Learning?" Presentation, September 14. www.slideshare.net /bchapman_utah/how-long-does-it-take-to-create-learning.

Cooper, A., R. Reimann, D. Cronin, and C. Noessel. 2014. *About Face: The Essentials of Interaction Design.* 4th ed. New York: Wiley.

Duarte, N. 2008. *slide:ology: The Art and Science of Creating Great Presentations.* Sebastopol, CA: O'Reilly Media.

Gagne, R.M. 1985. *The Conditions of Learning and Theory of Instruction.* 4th ed. New York: Holt, Rinehart, and Winston.

Hackos, J.T. 1994. *Managing Your Documentation Projects.* New York: Wiley.

Hartley, J. 2013. *Designing Instructional Text.* 3rd ed. London: Routledge.

Kapp, K., and R.A. Defelice. 2009. "Time to Develop One Hour of Training." Learning Circuits Newsletter, August 31. www.astd.org/Publications/Newsletters/Learning-Circuits/Learning-Circuits-Archives/2009/08/Time-to -Develop-One-Hour-of-Training.

Kirkpatrick, D.L. 1994. *Evaluating Training Programs: The Four Levels.* San Francisco, CA: Berrett-Koehler.

Kirschner, P.A., J. Sweller, and R.E. Clark. 2006. "Why Minimal Guidance During Instruction Does Not Work: An Analysis of the Failure of Constructivist, Discovery, Problem-Based, Experiential, and Inquiry-Based Teaching." *Educational Psychologist* 41(2): 75-86.

Knowles, M.S. 1973. *The Adult Learner: A Neglected Species.* Houston, TX: Gulf Publishing Company.

Knowles, M.S., E.F. Holton, and R.A. Swanson. 2011. *The Adult Learner: The Definitive Classic in Adult Education and Human Resource Development.* New York: Routledge.

Luiten, J., W. Ames, and G. Ackerson. 1980. "A Meta-Analysis of the Effects of Advance Organizers on Learning and Retention." *American Educational Research Journal* 17(2): 211-218.

Mager, R. 1997. *Preparing Instructional Objectives.* Atlanta, GA: Center for Effective Performance.

Masie, E. 2005. "Keynote Presentation." ALEGRO E-Learning Conference, Ottawa Council on Research and Innovation, September 14.

Price, D.W. 2013. "Improve PowerPoint by Trashing the Bullet Points." Presentation at e.SCAPE: The Conference on Knowledge, Teaching, and Technology, Concordia University, Montreal, April 4.

Price, J., and L. Price. 2002. *Hot Text: Web Writing That Works.* Indianapolis, IN: New Riders Press.

Robinson, D.G., and J. Robinson. 1989. *Training for Impact: How to Link Training to Business Needs and Measure Results.* 2nd ed. San Francisco, CA: Pfeiffer.

Schriver, K.A. 1996. *Dynamics in Document Design: Creating Text for Readers.* New York: Wiley.

van der Geest, T., and J.H. Spyridakis. 2000. "Developing Heuristics for Web Communication: An Introduction to This Special Issue." *Technical Communication* 47(3): 301-310.

Van der Meij, H., J. Karreman, and M. Steehouder. 2009. "Three Decades of Research and Professional Practice on Printed Software Tutorials for Novices." *Technical Communication* 56(3): 265-292.

Wurman, R.S. 1989. *Information Anxiety.* New York: Doubleday.

Additional Resources

Chapter 1

To learn more about:

Andragogy, read Malcolm S. Knowles, Elwood F. Holton, and Richard A. Swanson's *The Adult Learner: The Definitive Classic in Adult Education and Human Resource Development.* (2015). New York: Routledge.

Human performance improvement, read Harold D. Stolovitch and Erica J. Keeps's *Training Ain't Performance.* (2006). Alexandria, VA: ASTD Press.

Chapter 2

To learn more about:

The instructional systems design process in general, read Walter Dick, Lou Carey, and James O. Carey's *The Systematic Design of Instruction,* 8th edition. (2014). Upper Saddle River, NJ: Pearson.

Project management, read Karen Overfield's *Developing and Managing Organizational Learning: A Guide to Effective Training Project Management.* (2006). Alexandria, VA: ASTD Press.

Chapter 3

To learn more about:

Needs analysis in general, read Allison Rossett's *First Things Fast: A Handbook for Performance Analysis,* 2nd edition. (2009). San Francisco, CA: Pfeiffer.

Developing scenarios and personas, as well as a "design" mentality, read Alan Cooper and colleagues' *About Face: The Essentials of Interaction Design,* 4th edition. (2014). New York: Wiley.

Clarifying the goals of an instructional program, read Robert F. Mager's *Goal Analysis,* 3rd edition. (1997). Atlanta, GA: CEP Press.

Chapter 4

To learn more about:

Writing instructional objectives, read Robert F. Mager's classic, *Preparing Instructional Objectives,* 3rd edition. (1997). Atlanta: CEP Press.

Evaluating training programs, read either Donald Kirkpatrick's *Evaluating Training Programs: The Four Levels,* 3rd edition. (2006). San Francisco, CA: Berrett-Koehler; or Richard A. Swanson and Elwood F. Holton's *Results: How to Assess Performance, Learning, and Perceptions in Organizations.* (1999). San Francisco, CA: Berrett-Koehler.

Writing tests, read Robert F. Mager's related classic, *Measuring Instructional Results,* 3rd edition. (1997). Atlanta: CEP Press.

Chapter 5

To learn more about:

Designing for the live virtual classroom, check out Cindy Huggett's *Virtual Training Basics.* (2010). Alexandria, VA: ASTD Press—another book in ATD's Training Basics series.

Designing courses for self-study e-learning, check out William Horton's *E-Learning by Design.* (2011). San Francisco, CA: Pfeiffer; and, for more advanced techniques, Margaret Driscoll and my *Advanced Web-Based Training: Unlocking Instructionally Sound Online Learning.* (2005). San Francisco, CA: Pfeiffer.

Chapter 6

To learn more about:

The research and theory underlying instructional strategies, review Charles M. Reigeluth's classic *Instructional-Design Theories and Models: A New Paradigm of Instructional Theory.* (1999) Mahwah, NJ: Lawrence Erlbaum Associates.

Applications of research in training practice, read Ruth Colvin Clark's *Evidence-Based Training Methods,* 2nd edition. (2014). Alexandria, VA: ATD Press.

Chapter 7

To learn more about:

Creating programs with Microsoft PowerPoint, read Jane Bozarth's *Better Than Bullet Points: Creating Engaging E-Learning With PowerPoint,* 2nd edition. (2013). San Francisco, CA: Pfeiffer.

Chapter 8

To learn more about:

General approaches to instructing in a learner-centered way, check out Julie Dirksen's *Design for How People Learn.* (2012). Indianapolis, IN: New Riders.

Clearly written material, read William Strunk Jr. and E.B. White's *The Elements of Style,* 4th edition. (2000). Upper Saddle River, NJ: Pearson; or William Zinsser's *On Writing Well 30th Anniversary Edition: The Classic Guide to Writing Nonfiction.* (2006). New York: Harper Perennial.

Designing pages, read Robin Williams's *The Non-Designer's Design Book,* 4th edition. (2014). Berkeley, CA: Peachpit Press.

Chapter 9

To learn more about:

Editing, read Karen Judd's *Copyediting, A Practical Guide,* 3rd edition. (2001). Menlo Park, CA: Crisp Publications; or Marjorie E. Skillin and Robert M. Gay's classic, *Words Into Type.* (1974). Upper Saddle River, NJ: Pearson.

Planning a formative evaluation, consult Martin Tessmer's classic, *Planning and Conducting Formative Evaluations.* (1993). London, UK: Routledge.

Chapter 10

To learn more about:

Training administration and marketing, read Jean Barbazette's *The Trainer's Support Handbook: A Guide to Managing the Administrative Details of Training.* (2001). New York: McGraw-Hill.

Pricing, marketing, and managing various processes associated with implementing training programs, check out The Commerce of Content, my website about the business of training and development: http://commerceofcontent.wordpress.com.

About the Author

Saul Carliner is an associate professor of educational technology and provost's fellow for digital learning at Concordia University in Montreal. Also an industry consultant, he provides strategic plans, evaluations, designs, and workshops for clients such as Alltel Wireless, the Bronx Zoo, Lowe's, PwC, and several U.S. and Canadian government agencies.

Among his more than 200 publications are the international award-winning books, *Designing E-Learning* (ASTD 2006), *Informal Learning Basics* (ASTD 2012), and *The e-Learning Handbook: A Comprehensive Guide to Online Learning* (Pfeiffer 2008) with Patti Shank.

He has received the 2014 Ken Rainey Award for Excellence in Research, the 2014 Jay Gould Award for Teaching from the Society for Technical Communication, and the 2014 Alumni Award for Excellence in Teaching from his university. He is a fellow and past international president of the Society for Technical Communication, a past research fellow of ATD, and a fellow and a past board member of the Canadian Society for Training and Development. A long-time community leader, Carliner has chaired a museum membership auxiliary; civic transit board; several allocations committees for community foundations; and served on boards of several arts, professional, and community organizations.

HOW TO PURCHASE ATD PRESS PUBLICATIONS

ATD Press publications are available worldwide in print and electronic format.

To place an order, please visit our online store: www.td.org/books.

Our publications are also available at select online and brick-and-mortar retailers.

Outside the United States, English-language ATD Press titles may be purchased through the following distributors:

**United Kingdom, Continental Europe,
the Middle East, North Africa, Central Asia,
Australia, New Zealand, and Latin America**
Eurospan Group
Phone: 44.1767.604.972
Fax: 44.1767.601.640
Email: eurospan@turpin-distribution.com
Website: www.eurospanbookstore.com

Asia
Cengage Learning Asia Pte. Ltd.
Phone: (65)6410-1200
Email: asia.info@cengage.com
Website: www.cengageasia.com

Nigeria
Paradise Bookshops
Phone: 08033075133
Email: paradisebookshops@gmail.com
Website: www.paradisebookshops.com

South Africa
Knowledge Resources
Phone: +27 (11) 706.6009
Fax: +27 (11) 706.1127
Email: sharon@knowres.co.za
Web: www.kr.co.za

For all other territories, customers may place their orders at the ATD online store:
www.td.org/books.

0215145.62220